100 WAL.

Derbyshire

The Crowood Press

First published in 1990 by
The Crowood Press Ltd
Ramsbury, Marlborough
Wiltshire SN8 2HR

Revised edition 1997

British Library Cataloguing in Publication Data
A catalogue record for this book
is available from the British Library

ISBN 1 86126 077 6

Maps by Philip Smith and Allan Williams

Typeset by Carreg Limited, Ross-on-Wye, Herefordshire

Printed and bound in Great Britain by
J W Arrowsmith Ltd, Bristol

THE CONTRIBUTORS

Stan Coe

Janet Forrest

Tony Kershaw

A J Middleton

A E Parkes

David Robinson

Malcolm Sales

CONTENTS

South-West

South-East

32. and shorter version
33. Quarndon and Kedleston $7^1/_2$m (12km)
34. Around Milford 12m (19km)

North-East

35. Hall Dale 3m (5km)
36. Stone Edge and Holymoorside 3m (5km)
37. Padley Gorge $3^3/_4$m (6km)
38. Northern Chatsworth $4^1/_2$m (7km)
39. Matlock and Bonsall 5m (8km)
40. Matlock and Wensley Dale 6m (9.5km)
41. Holymoorside and Old Brampton 7m (11.5km)
42. The Hope Valley 7m (11km)
43. Around Somersall Park 7m (11km)
44. Ashover and Littlemoor 7m (11km)
45. Linacre Woods and Millthorpe $8^1/_4$m (13km)

North-West

46. Bakewell $1^1/_2$m (2.5km)
47. Middle Moor $3^1/_4$m (5km)
48. Stanton Moor $3^1/_2$m (5.5km)
49. Higger Tor and Carl Wark $3^1/_2$m (5.5km)
50. Edale and Mam Tor $3^1/_2$m (5.5km)
51. Darley Dale and Sydnope Dale 4m (6.5km)
52. Deepdale from Chelmorton 4m (6.5km)
53. Cressbrook Dale $4^1/_2$m (7km)
54. Flash $4^1/_2$m (7km)
55. Solomon's Temple $4^1/_2$m (7km)
56. Longnor and Earl Sterndale $4^1/_2$m (7km)
57. Chatsworth Park and Beeley Moor 5m (8km)
58. Baslow and Birchen Edge 5m (8km)
59. Great Shacklow Wood 5m (8km)
60. Elton and Birchover $5^1/_2$m (9km)
61. Baslow and Curbar $5^1/_2$m (9km)
62. Longstone Moor 6m (9.5km)
63. Brown Knoll 6m (9.5km)
64. Hartington and Beresford 6m (9.5km)

65. Castleton and Lose Hill 6m (9.5km)
66. Around Hathersage 6$\frac{1}{2}$m (10.5km)
67. Earl Sterndale and Hollinsclough 7m (11km)
68. Win Hill and Ladybower 7m (11km)
69. Bakewell and Edensor 7m (11km)
70. The Northern Edge of Kinder Scout 7m (11km)
71. Sir William Hill and Eyam Moor 7m (11km)
72. Edale and Jacob's Ladder 7$\frac{1}{2}$m (12km)
73. Cock Hill and Torside 7$\frac{1}{2}$m (12km)
74. Hathersage and Stanage Edge 7$\frac{1}{2}$m (12km)
75. Tideswell and Cressbrook 7$\frac{1}{2}$m (12km)
76. Longshaw Lodge 7$\frac{1}{2}$m (12km)
77. Axe Edge Moor 7$\frac{1}{2}$m (12km)
78. Calton Lees and Rowsley 8m (13km)
79. Grinah Stones 8m (13km)
80. Stony Middleton and Eyam 8m (13km)
81. Rocking Stones and Howden Clough 8m (13km)
82. Upper Dovedale 8m (13km)
83. Kinder Scout 8m (13km)
84. Around Elton 9m (14.5km)
85. Hope and Castleton 9m (14.5km)
86. Windgather Rocks 9m (14.5km)
87. Monsal Head and Monsal Dale 9m (14.5km)
88. Ladybower and Derwent Edge 9m (14.5km)
89. Alport Castles 9m (14.5km)
90. Mam Tor and Rushup Edge 9m (14.5km)
91. Kinder Scout and Mount Famine 9m (14.5km)
92. Longdendale 9m (14.5km)
93. Bakewell and Youlgreave 10m (16km)
94. Monyash to Chelmorton 10m (16km)
95. Hathersage and Stony Middleton 10m (16km)
96. Alport and Elton 10m (16km)
97. Rowsley and Stanton Moor 10m (16km)
98. Back Tor 11m (17.5km)
99. Darley Bridge and Winster 11m (17.5km)
100. Lathkill Dale 12m (19km)

PUBLISHER'S NOTE

We very much hope that you enjoy the routes presented in this book, which has been compiled with the aim of allowing you to explore the area in the best possible way - on foot.

We strongly recommend that you take the relevant map for the area, and for this reason we list the appropriate Ordnance Survey maps for each route. Whilst the details and descriptions given for each walk were accurate at time of writing, the countryside is constantly changing, and a map will be essential if, for any reason, you are unable to follow the given route. It is good practice to carry a map and use it so that you are always aware of your exact location.

We cannot be held responsible if some of the details in the route descriptions are found to be inaccurate, but should be grateful if walkers would advise us of any major alterations. Please note that whenever you are walking in the countryside you are on somebody else's land, and we must stress that you should *always* keep to established rights of way, and *never* cross fences, hedges or other boundaries unless there is a clear crossing point.

Remember the country code:

Enjoy the country and respect its life and work
Guard against all risk of fire
Fasten all gates
Keep dogs under close control
Keep to public footpaths across all farmland
Use gates and stiles to cross field boundaries
Leave all livestock, machinery and crops alone
Take your litter home
Help to keep all water clean
Protect wildlife, plants and trees
Make no unnecessary noise

The walks are listed by length - from approximately 1 to 12 miles - but the amount of time taken will depend on the fitness of the walkers and the time spent exploring any points of interest along the way. Nearly all the walks are circular and most offer recommendations for refreshments.

Good walking.

NOTE

Not unexpectedly, many of the walks in this volume are in the Peak District National Park. They are, therefore, routes through high and remote countryside where the weather can alter dramatically and where the terrain can tax even the fittest. If you intend to do one of these walks, it is essential that you are always in possession of and are able to use a map and compass. In addition, you must be adequately equipped. Boots are recommended for most upland walks; not only is the going frequently wet but it is also likely that the path is rough. Waterproof clothing is advised. It is better to carry it all day unused than to be caught far from shelter without it.

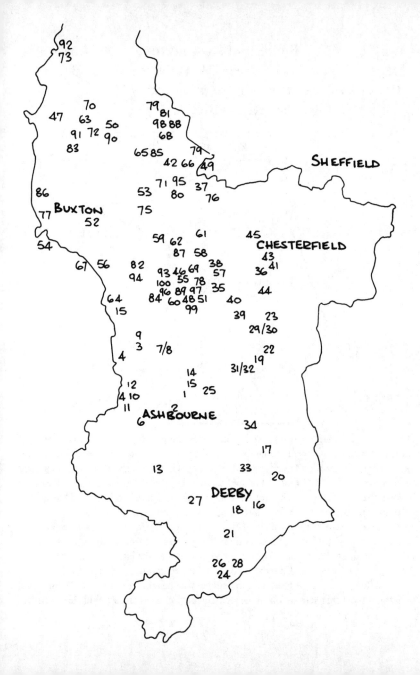

Walk 1   **BIGGIN AND KIRK IRETON**   4m (6.5km)

Maps: OS Sheets Landranger 119; Pathfinder SK 24/34.

A short walk with some very steep ascents.

Start: At 261486, the green in Biggin.

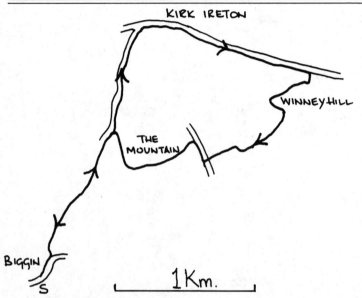

From the green walk down to the T-junction by the post box. Go straight on through the five bar gate and over the stile. Go down the field beyond to a bridge. Continue over a stile, cross a track and go over the double stile. Go to the left of the large sheds and up the field to a stile. Go across the field bearing slightly left to a stile. Follow the hedge down the field and where it turns left continue straight on to a bridge over the stream. Go over the double fence and continue uphill. Pass to the left of the farm and turn left on to a track. After going through a gateway, turn right and follow the track uphill. After $^1/_2$ mile turn right at the road and continue straight on towards Kirk Ireton for 100 yards to a right turn to Idridgehay. The Barley Mow pub is on the left. Continue through the village, past the post office stores and follow the road towards Idridgehay.

After 1 mile, at the bottom of the hill past the bench, turn right into Winney Hill Farm. Just before the farm follow the sign to a footpath and follow uphill along a hedge.

14

Pass through a gateway and turn right. Follow the hedge to the top of the hill. Cross a stile, go through a gate and again follow a hedge. Cross a stile and follow the edge of the field round to the road. Turn right. After 100 yards take the track to the left. Cross the stile next to the gate and continue to a gateway. Pass just to the left of bushes and follow the path downhill and around 'the Mountain'. Turn left over a stile and on reaching a track turn left. At a fork, go left and down the field to the right of the farm. Now follow the path down, going over a double fence and a bridge and then up a field. Cross a stile and go to the right of the large sheds. Cross the stile in the corner of the field, go over the track and down the next field to another stile. Go over, and then over a bridge, up the field and over a stile. Go through a gate to the road and over the road opposite. Follow the road back to the start point.

REFRESHMENTS:
The Barley Mow Pub, Kirk Ireton (tel no: 0335 70306). A 17th-century pub with a beer garden.

Walk 2   **HULLAND WARD AND HULLAND**   4m (6.5km)
Maps: OS Sheets Landranger 119; Pathfinder SK 24/34.
A short walk with some streams and marshy areas.
Start: At 261469, the Black Horse Inn, Hulland Ward.

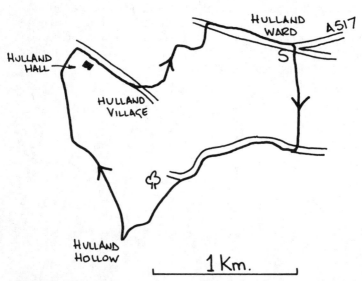

From the front of the inn walk towards Hulland Ward to reach a footpath on the left at
'High Meadow'. Follow this path for $^1/_2$ mile to a lane. Turn right into Hulland Village
and continue to 'Moss Farmhouse'. Turn left here and follow a track down a field,
turning right when the track forks. Cross a stile and go downhill diagonally across the
field to the bottom right-hand corner. Cross the stream and walk down a field to a
bridge, keeping the stream to your left. Cross the bridge and go through a gap in the
hedge ahead. Turn right and follow the hedge along the edge of a field. Cross a bridge
and continue left for about 100 yards. Take the path to the left, fording the stream.
Continue along the centre of the sheltered valley through a marshy area for $^1/_4$ mile until
you reach a track. Follow this up the hill to the right. Go through a stream and over a
stile. Turn right and keep to the edge of the woods until Hulland Hall is seen ahead.
Follow the line of trees across fields to a track, and turn right to walk between Hulland

Hall and Old Hall to The Green. Turn right and enter Hulland Village. After $^1/_4$ mile the entrance to a farm will be passed. Just after this take the footpath to the left. Follow it for 100 yards then turn left over a stile. Follow the stepping stones across the stream and walk up the field. Pass through a gap in the hedge, go over a ditch and up the left-hand side of a field. Go through the hedge and turn right to the opposite corner of the field. Go across the next field, over a double stile and left towards houses. The footpath meets the road next to the Nag's Head pub. Turn right along the road and the Black Horse Inn is $^1/_4$ mile ahead.

REFRESHMENTS:
The Black Horse Inn, Hulland Ward (tel no: 0335 703206). Old beamed pub. Lunchtime carvery, evening meals. Beer garden.
The Nag's Head, Hulland Ward (tel no: 0335 70217).

Walk 3   **TISSINGTON AND FENNY BENTLEY** $4^1/_2$m (7km)

Maps: OS Sheets Landranger 119; Outdoor Leisure 24.

An easy walk with no difficult stretches.

Start: At 177521, Tissington Trail car park in Tissington.

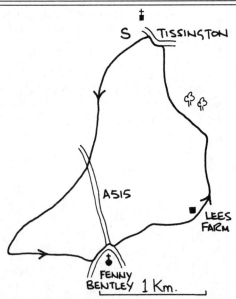

Leave the car park and follow the **Tissington Trail** south. After $^3/_4$ mile the trail passes over the A515 on an old railway bridge and then continues for another $^3/_4$ mile to what was once Thorpe Cloud Station. Just after the station is a footpath off to the left signposted 'Fenny Bentley'. Take this. Go through the gate and down fields, bearing slightly left to cross a bridge over the stream. Go directly ahead, up the hill and across the field to a stile. Follow the path, keeping the hedge to the right. After the next stile cross a field, keeping to the centre. Fenny Bentley can be seen below. Go through a gate at the bottom of the field and down to a lane. Turn left and follow the lane to the main road, passing the church of St Edmund. Cross the main road and follow the path to the right for a few yards until a footpath can be seen, going off left, by a phone box. A short distance further along the main road is the Coach and Horses pub if refreshment is required.

Follow the path alongside the stream for a few yards and then go through the ford. There is a bridge just to the left if required. Go over the stile next o the gate ahead. Cross a field following the line of telephone poles, to a gate on the right-hand side. Cross the next field, passing between the hedge and the barn to a stile. Pass through the next three fields and join the tarmac road at the V-junction. Take the right fork uphill through the farmyard. After 100 yards there is a signpost for Tissington and Parwich. Follow the Tissington arrow over a stile and up a field to the top left-hand corner. Go over a stile and up the next field bearing slightly left to the top left-hand corner. Go through the stile and follow the hedge round to the left to a stile and gate. Cross the next field keeping to the left and after a stile cross the next field to the diagonally opposite corner, passing behind a ruined barn. Go through a gate and over a cattle grid. Continue along the tarmac road to a lane and turn left towards **Tissington**. The car park start is on the left as you enter the village.

POINTS OF INTEREST:

Tissington Trail – A disused railway line, once part of the London and North Western Railway. This section ran between Ashbourne and Buxton, and was finally closed in 1963.

Tissington – The village famous for the 'dressing' of its five wells on Ascension Day.

REFRESHMENTS:

The Coach and Horses, Fenny Bentley (tel no: 033 529 246). Country pub with beer garden and restaurant.

Maps: OS Sheets Landranger 119; Pathfinder SK 04/14 & 14/15.

A fine walk combining river and country walking.

Start: At 131507, the car park in the grounds of Ilam Hall.

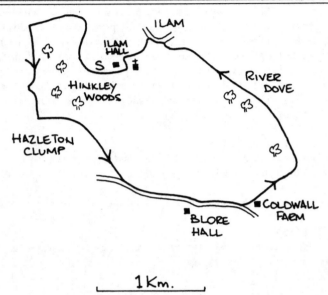

Follow the terraced riverside path and turn left over a footbridge. Do not take the main path on the right but go uphill towards the woods on the skyline. Go over a stile in a broken down wall and turn left to follow a wall and grassy track. Cross a valley to reach a track which curves right and uphill around Hazleton Clump. Go over a stile and turn left along a road. Follow the road over a crossroads to reach Coldwall Farm. Leave the road and go through the farmyard to a field. Go downhill towards the river. This section of the walk follows the old turnpike road from Staffordshire to Yorkshire. Go left along a fence before reaching Coldwall Bridge, and go through a gap in it to reach the bank. Follow the bank to reach steps to a bridge. Turn right at the top and go along the road to **Ilam** village. Turn left beyond Dovedale House following the church path back to **Ilam Hall** and its car park.

POINTS OF INTEREST:

Ilam – The village dates back to Saxon times. St Bertram, a Saxon hermit, had a cell near where the river re-surfaced close to the hall. The church dedicated to the saint was much altered in the 1930s when the village was rebuilt by Jesse Watts Russell.

Ilam Hall – Little now remains of the original building, most having been demolished in the early 1930s. The rest was also to be pulled down but was bought by Sir Robert McDougall, a Manchester businessman, who rebuilt it and gave it to the National Trust. It is now a youth hostel.

REFRESHMENTS:

There is a café in the grounds of Ilam Hall.

Walk 5   WOLFSCOTE DALE AND NARROW DALE   5m (8km)

Maps: OS Sheets Landranger 119; Outdoor Leisure 24.

A good walk along the River Dove and back through a little-known valley.

Start: At 128586, Beaver Ford.

Go over the footbridge and turn right. Ignore the next footbridge, staying on the path through the gorge of Wolfscote Dale to reach the entrance to Biggin Dale. About 200 yards ahead now are **Stepping Stones** over the Dove.

Beyond is a path to a stile. Go over and left towards a barn. Join a track here and follow it to a junction. Go left and down to a road. Go right into **Alstonefield**. The George Inn is on the left. Keep right and follow the road, signed 'Hulme End', for 400 yards to an obvious left-hand bend. Go over a stile on the right, go right and cross a field towards the corner of a small wood. Go over a track and follow a footpath over several stiles to reach a stile in the wall on the right. Go over and down into Narrow Dale. Follow the path through it to a track. Go over to a track which leads back to the start.

22

POINTS OF INTEREST:

Stepping Stones – The river near these stones was the favourite haunt of Izaak Walton the 17th-century fisherman who wrote *The Compleat Angler*. It is also a good place to see dippers.

Alstonefield – The Elizabethan Manor House is 16th century. The three-storey house by the Post Office was once the Workhouse.

REFRESHMENTS:

The George Inn, Alstonefield (tel no: 033 527 205).
There is also a tea shop in Alstonefield.

Walk 6   **OSMASTON**   5m (8km)

Maps: OS Sheets Landranger 119; Pathfinder SK 04/14 & 24/34.

An undulating walk through fields and woods.

Start: At 199439, the car park, Osmaston village hall.

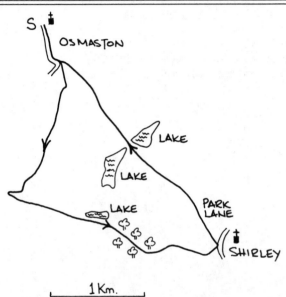

Turn right from the car park to pass left of the village pond and along a drive with a lodge
on the left. Go first right along a minor road through trees to a sharp left-hand bend. Here
turn right to a gate and a rough track. Follow this through a second gate to the bottom
corner of a field and then turn right to a third gate. Go through this and swing left to a
path near the boundary and, after crossing three stiles, take the lake-side path to the end
of the lake.Continue straight ahead through a gate and along the waymarked woodland
path to a gate at the far side of the wood. Turn left and, shortly, cross a footbridge and
a stile, opposite, to walk along the right field boundary for 140 yards to a stile. Cross
this and head diagonally left across the field to a stile by a gate. Go over and after 120
yards cross another stile on the left and turn right to walk along two sides of a field to
a double stile. Go over and follow the short path and steps down to a road. Turn left
along a tarmac access road which becomes a rough bridleway. Follow this for about

two miles, ignoring all turnings, back to **Osmaston** and the start of the walk near the village hall.

POINTS OF INTEREST:
Osmaston – An attractive estate village. The thatched cottage near the pond is an excellent example of 'cruck' construction.

REFRESHMENTS:
The Saracens Head, Shirley (tel no: 0335 60330).
The Shoulder of Mutton, Osmaston (tel no: 0335 42371).

Walks 7 and 8   **BRADBOURNE AND KNIVETON**   5m (8km)
Maps: OS Sheets Landranger 119; Outdoor Leisure 24.
An easy walk over undulating countryside.
Start: At 208527, near the church in Bradbourne.

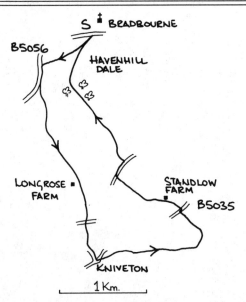

Take the footpath at the western end of the village. Follow the pointer to the first stile where you continue straight ahead (the right-hand fork on the map) crossing a field track to the next stile. Go down through the next field to the road (B5056). Turn left. A short way on, at the ford to your right, take a track – actually a county road – going up hill on your left. From here, the walk is characterised by the small iron gates, courtesy of Kniveton Parish Council. Beyond the first of these the track becomes walled. Just past a barn look for another gate on the left. Go through this and head diagonally over the field through a gap in a line of trees. A path now leads easily to Longrose Farm. At the farm the way is a little to your left rather than ahead through the farm as it is shown on the map. Continue through four more gates on the road, cross over and carry on to the field before the caravan site where you turn right through a gate half-way down. This path leads to **Kniveton** where you emerge next to the Red Lion.

Go down the road straight opposite and turn left just past a telephone box. Go through a large gate, past houses, through a 'garden' gate and a footpath gate. Cross the field to another small gate then bear right gradually towards the brook. Go left up hill and under the power line to reach a track. Here there is a double signpost. Take the path for Hognaston. After two small gates the path crosses (half-way along the next field) through a gateway to the other side of the hedge. Follow the hedge to its end then bear left over a field to a fenced plantation ahead (not shown on the map). Turn left along the fence to a stone stile. Continue through the plantation a short way on to a track. Turn left and continue down the track to the main road (B5035). From the track you have a good view of Thorpe Cloud to the west, the hill at the southern end of Dove Dale. Cross the road and turn right for a few yards to another lane opposite. Follow this past Standlow Farm then, where the lane turns left down into Kniveton, go through a gate on the right and keeping in line with the lane you have left follow this (unused) bridleway through two more gates on to a lane. Turn right for a short way then left through a small gate into a dry dale. There is a good view of Parwich from here. Follow the dale down to Havenhill Dale Brook at the bottom. Cross the brook by the right-hand of two foot bridges then go over the next bridge and up the bank to a stile on your right. Go diagonally over the field up to a stile midway along the opposite hedge. Continue in the same direction to another stile and the road at **Bradbourne.**

This walk may be shortened by about 1 mile by turning left along the road at Kniveton then left again at Closes Farm to reach the dale path.

POINTS OF INTEREST:
Kniveton – Hereward Street, a Roman road, ran along the present road through Kniveton linking the Roman station at Rocester with the fort at Chesterfield.
Bradbourne – It is worth walking round this village and visiting the church with its impressive large Norman tower.

REFRESHMENTS:
The Red Lion, Kniveton (tel no: 0335 45554).

Walk 9   **TISSINGTON AND PARWICH**   5m (8km)

Maps: OS Sheets Landranger 119; Outdoor Leisure 24.

A relatively easy walk through pleasantly undulating countryside.

Start: At 176522, the car park at the old railway station, Tissington.

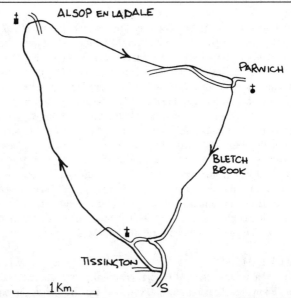

Turn left from the car park and walk past the village pond. Turn right up the main street to a sharp left turn. A footpath sign points the way to Alsop across fields. Follow the line of stiles across four fields to arrive at a pair of gates in the far-left corner of the fifth field. Go through the right-hand gate, over two wall stiles and pass just to the right of farm buildings to reach a stile in the field corner. Go over and turn right along the farm track. After passing under an old railway bridge, cross three stiles and head for the left boundary wall at the top of the rise. Cross a stile and turn immediately right over a second stile and then head diagonally left to a stile at the edge of the trees. Go over and descend to the left-corner of the field and a wall stile. Go over and make a line to the right-hand side of the farm buildings, noting **Alsop-en-la-Dale** Church and Hall to the left.

After crossing a wall stile and a farmyard, reach a road over another stile. Turn

28

right and then left quite soon over a stile at the corner of a cottage garden. Go over and diagonally left, over two wall stiles, to the bottom of the wood. Follow a clear path through the wood to the far side. Keep ahead over five fields crossing stiles. Cross a farm drive to a hedge stile just left of the far-right corner of the field. Go over and straight across a farm drive. Cross two more stiles to reach a road via a stile in a fence to the left of the drive entrance. Two hundred yards down the road turn left by the signpost and walk up the pathway to follow a clear line across a series of narrow fields to Parwich village. Pass in front of the houses along a tarmac path, turning right at the junction with a road and then left on a footpath for Tissington. (To visit Parwich go left along the brookside path.) Follow the direction of the sign along a clear line up the hill and over a series of stiles and a footbridge. Descend the hillside to cross a footbridge over Bletch brook and then climb to the signpost ahead at the top of the hill. Go left here along a farm track, over a railway bridge and turn first left along the narrow lane which takes you back to Tissington (see Walk 4) and the start.

POINTS OF INTEREST:
Alsop-en-la-Dale – Some parts of the original Norman church remain. The Hall is 17th century.

REFRESHMENTS:
The Sycamore Inn, Parwich (tel no: 033 525 212).

Walk 10   THORPE CLOUD AND MAPLETON   6m (9.5km)

Maps: OS Sheets Landranger 119; Pathfinder SK 04/14.

A well-marked route with no difficult sections.

Start: At 147509, the car park at Dove Dale.

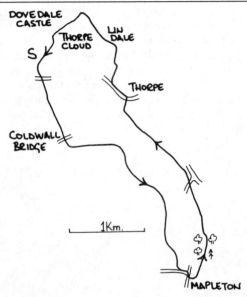

Follow the footpath alongside the stream. At the road turn left, then take the footpath off to the right. Cross the stile ahead and follow the small dike around, keeping it to your right. At the main stream turn left and continue to follow the left bank. At the stone bridge cross over the track and follow the track ahead. Go through the farmyard and continue along the left-hand side of the field, over a stile and along the river. Cross straight over the road by the bridge and follow the path across a field to the Okeover Arms. Turn right on to the road and left on to a footpath signposted 'Ashbourne'. Follow the path between hedges and at the field turn left. Go through a gap in the hedge, then cross the next field diagonally right and follow the hedge ahead round to the left. Go over a stile and cross a field, going just to the right of the gate seen ahead. Go over a stile and follow the left-hand edge of the wood. Go through a gate into the woods and follow the path to another gate. Cross the stile on the left of the gate and turn right to follow the edge of the field. **Thorpe Cloud**, the highest point in the area, can be seen ahead.

Keep along the hedge to a road junction. Turn right and, in a few yards, take the footpath signposted 'Dove Dale'. Follow the right-hand hedge to a sign pointing across a field, and cross to a stile. Turn left as signposted, cross the next stile and turn right. Keep to the left of the stone wall. Cross a farm track, continuing to follow the stone wall. Go down the valley towards the church seen ahead and cross a stile in the corner of a field by the bushes. Go up the opposite side of the valley, over a stile and turn left. Follow the path to the churchyard and turn right to meet the road. Turn right, and as the road forks go left. At the main road go straight over and follow a track past toilets. Now follow the track signposted 'Dove Dale' for 200 yards, then turn left to go down into Lin Dale. Pass to the right of Thorpe Cloud and follow the dale down to the river. Either cross the stepping stones and turn left here, or simply turn left and follow the nearside bank down to the car park.

POINTS OF INTEREST:
Thorpe Cloud – A steep hill and the highest point in the area. Many footpaths to the top. Excellent views when the weather is clear.

REFRESHMENTS:
The Okeover Arms, Mapleton (tel no: 033 529 305). Village pub, serving bar food.

Walk 11   **ASHBOURNE**   6m (9.5km)

Maps: OS Sheets Landranger 119; Pathfinder SK 04/14.

A relatively easy walk through pleasant scenery.

Start: At 175469, the car park at the Ashbourne end of the
Tissington Trail.

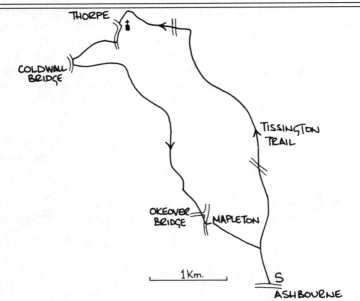

Walk up the Trail (the bed of the old Ashbourne to Buxton railway line) for two miles
and then turn left through a kissing gate by a signpost, 'Thorpe – Dove Dale'. Go
straight across two fields to the road 200 yards away, and cross straight over to a farm
track. Follow this past Broadlowash Farm and into **Thorpe** village.

  Take the first left turn and go up the road past the church to a gate, beyond which
is a track which was once part of the turnpike road from Cheadle in Staffordshire.
Descend the track, noting the old distance marker on the left , 'Cheadle II miles', to the
beginning of **Coldwall Bridge**. Turn left down a farm track, go over a stile and left
again to pass to the right of the farm house, as waymarked. Follow the left boundary
hedge to a stile. Now the path follows the River Dove closely until the river swings
sharp right towards a weir. The path goes straight on here, across the middle of a field,

and rejoins the river until the road is reached near Okeover Bridge. Cross the road and a stile. Go left across the corner of a field and exit on to the road adjacent to Okeover Arms. Just beyond the pub turn left up a path by a cottage to cross a stile into fields. Head diagonally right over two more stiles to follow the left boundary hedge round the corner to another stile. After crossing the stile veer right to follow the path on a straight line through stiles and fields to the Tissington Trail. Turn right to the car park, 400 yards away, where the walk began.

POINTS OF INTEREST:

Thorpe – A Danish settlement overlooking the entrance to Dove Dale. The church was originally Norman and has been little changed. Inside there are Elizabethan altar rails.
Coldwall Bridge – Was built in 1726 to carry the old turnpike road from Cheadle.

REFRESHMENTS:

The Dog and Partridge , Thorpe (tel no: 033 529 235).
The Okeover Arms, Mapleton (tel no: 033 529 305).

Walk 12   **Thorpe and Dove Dale**   6m (9.5km)

Maps: OS Sheets Landranger 119; Outdoor Leisure 24.

A steady climb to the hill top above Dove Dale. Beautiful views and a descent through Dove Dale.

Start: At 163503, the car park opposite the Dog and Partridge public house in Thorpe.

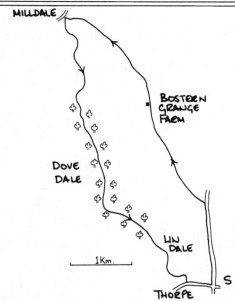

Turn right out of the car park and right again up a single track gated road. About 150 yards past the second gate cross a stile on the left by a signpost and walk diagonally right to a stile half way along the wall. Go over this and left to a gateway and a stile. Now follow the left boundary wall to another stile. From here the route crosses several fields in a fairly straight line to a small ladder stile at a wall corner. Cross and follow the wall to Bostern Grange. Continue straight ahead down the farmyard, over the drive and cross two stiles to reach the far wall and a signpost for Milldale. Turn left to the top of the field and cross a stile on to a rough track. Follow this across the farm drive. Follow the left-hand boundary on a steadily descending path to the final steep, zigzag descent to **Viator's Bridge** and Milldale.

34

From the bridge a firm path on the left-hand of the River Dove passes through beautiful Dove Dale to reach a stile just before the stepping stones across the river. Go through the stile, turn left to a kissing gate and follow the path up Lin Dale swinging right on the hillside to a track at the top going right to the village. Cross the track and follow the right boundary wall to a stile. Go over this and cross two narrow fields to the road. Turn left to arrive back at the car park where the walk began.

POINTS OF INTEREST:

Viator's Bridge – An old packhorse bridge called after Viator (traveller) from Essex who is referred to in the 5th edition (1676) of *The Compleat Angler* by Izaak Walton.

REFRESHMENTS:

The Dog and Partridge, Thorpe (tel no: 033 529 235).
Milldale has a small shop and café serving light snacks.

Walk 13   **LONGFORD**   7m (11km)

Maps: OS Sheets Landranger 128; Pathfinder SK 23/33.

Magnificent views across East Derbyshire.

Start: At 213378, Long Lane, Longford. Please park with care in the village.

Walk northwards along the lane leading to Longford Hall Farm. Across the park you will see **Longford Hall**. At a row of cottages, turn right to **St Chad's Church**. Now, by the church, turn left and pass the well-kept brick stable yard. Follow the lane through the farm yard and across a field to reach a road. Cross the road and go through a metal gate into a field. Cross this grassy field, heading north-east towards woodland. Go over a stile into the wood and cross a wooden bridge over a stream. The path now continues north-eastwards, uphill, across fields, passing a brick barn. Finally the path follows a hedgerow into Hollington, going through the garden of Meadow View Cottage. Look for the old-fashioned water pump in the garden.

Turn right to reach the Red Lion Inn. Footpaths exit opposite both the Red Lion and Meadow View Cottage: either of these will take you across grassy fields to reach

Slade Hollow Lane, thus bypassing the village. Walk down the lane for 500 yards to reach a signed bridleway on the right. Follow this bridleway, walking with a hedge on your left, to reach a gate. Go through, turn left and walk beside the hedge to reach the next hedge. Go over a stile and turn right, walking along the edge of a grassy field to reach a gate. Turn left and walk beside a hedge to reach a wooden bridge crossing Brailsford Brook.

The path beyond the bridge crosses arable fields to reach Long Lane. Cross and go along the lane opposite, following it to a T-junction. Turn left to reach the quaint hamlet of Thurvaston. Turn first right and follow the road for 300 yards to reach a signed footpath on the left. Go over the stile and cross the arable field beyond, and then several grassy fields, following the Bonnie Prince Charlie walk to reach a road near Osleston.

Turn right and follow the road through Osleston to reach a T-junction. Turn right along Back Lane to reach a cross roads at Windle Hill Farm, near a beautiful duck pond. Turn right and walk to another crossroads. Go straight across and follow a track to a sharp left bend. Here, bear left (north-westwards) along an unmade farm drive, crossing a cattle grid. At the entrance to the farm, go left to reach a gate in a hedge. Go through and walk with a hedgerow on your right, passing from field to field as you follow a path towards the thatched, Tudor-looking, Sharrow Hall in Lower Thurvaston. Cross a road to another footpath beside Marsh Farm and follow it across two fields to reach a road close to the village sign for **Longford**. Turn right and follow the road into the village to return to the start of the walk, crossing Sutton Brook and passing the old water mill, now a private residence.

POINTS OF INTEREST:
Longford Hall – Originally built in late medieval times, the Hall was the home of the Longford family. It passed to the Coke family and was 'reorganised' by the Pickfords in 1762.
St Chad's Church – There has been a church on this site since Saxon times. Inside the present building there are fine monuments to the Cokes and the Longfords.
Longford – Longford was the home of the first cheese factory in England. The factory was opened in 1870 under the managership of one Cornelius Schermerhorn.

REFRESHMENTS:
The Red Lion Inn, Hollington.

Walk 14   CARSINGTON RESERVOIR   8¹/₂m (13.75km)

Maps: OS Sheets Landranger 119; Pathfinder SK 24/34.

A hilly walk with some steep gradients.

Start: At 247497, the Millfields car park.

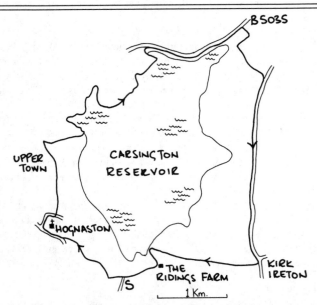

Take the footpath west from near the access road. Cross the road leading to the dam and continue to the bottom of the hill. Turn right, go over the fields and cross a bridge over a stream. Continue along the path near to the service road to meet the main road. Turn right, go over the bridge and up the hill into the village of Hognaston. Pass the Post Office Stores and both churches. Just after the second church, and before the Red Lion, turn right and follow a track down the hill, taking the right fork. Go left of the stream and follow the farm track to a gate. Go over the stile on your right and continue up the left-hand side of the field. Turn left at the lane and follow it through the farm to a road. Turn right here. In a few yards there is a stile on your left. Cross the stile, pass behind a barn and keep in a straight line to the edge of the reservoir. Follow the path left, around the edge of the reservoir past Shiningford Farm to a car park. Continue to the B5035 and turn right. This is the only main road on the walk: follow it for nearly 1 mile. There are good views of the reservoir and dam on the right. Just before the left turn to Hopton take the footpath on the right, next to a gate. Follow this up the hill for 100 yards, and then take the footpath on the left.

Continue south-east uphill across a field, keeping parallel to the woods on the right. At the top of the hill turn right on to a lane and follow it for $1^3/_4$ miles, passing through Callow to Kirk Ireton. On entering the village the Barley Mow pub is just around the bend to the left. Take the road signposted 'Blackwall and Hulland'. In a few yards, as the road forks, there is a footpath on the right by a gate. Take the path, keeping to the hedge on the right. After a stile, follow the hedge to the left until a road is reached. Go straight over and continue down a track signposted 'The Riddings Farm'. The reservoir will be seen directly ahead. Pass the farm on the left and, after 100 yards, turn left and follow the track to the car park.

REFRESHMENTS:
The Red Lion, Hognaston (tel no: 0335 70396). Small village pub.
The Barley Mow, Kirk Ireton (tel no: 0335 70306). 17th-century pub, unspoilt by modern life. Low beams, slate-topped tables and beer garden.

Walk 15   MILLDALE AND BIGGIN DALE   9m (14.5km)

Maps: OS Sheets Landranger 119; Outdoor Leisure 24.

The dales of the River Dove and the Tissington Trail.

Start: At 156548, the car park at Alsop Station on the Tissington Trail.

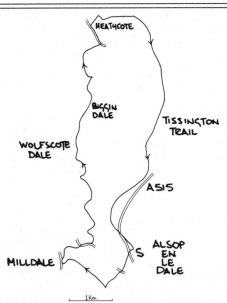

Return to the main road and go over a stile on the far side. Follow a path across a field to a minor road. Cross and go up the farm drive opposite. Cross a cattle grid and turn right at the path crossroads. Follow the left boundary on a clear path descending to Viator's Bridge (see Walk 12) and Milldale. Fine views of Staffordshire can be seen during the descent, with Alstonfield just across the dale. The River Dove forms part of the Derbyshire/Staffordshire boundary so by crossing the bridge you enter Staffordshire. As its name suggests, Milldale once had a mill and evidence of it still remains. Follow the road alongside the river to Lode Mill Bridge and enter Wolfscote Dale by a stile at the end of the bridge. The path meanders along the riverside through the dale, with its hills and limestone cliffs, for about 1^3/$_4$ miles to Biggin Dale. If you are lucky you may catch sight of a dipper walking underwater in search of food. Follow the right-hand

40

boundary wall up Biggin Dale, which is often dry with wild flowers growing on its slopes, to reach a gate, a stile and a National Trust sign. Go over the stile and continue, with the wall on your left, following a clear path to the top of the dale. Ignore paths going right and left. You pass a sewage works on your left before reaching the road at Dale End.

Go left up the road, and cross a stile on the right opposite a road junction. Follow the wall uphill to a stile. Go over and cross a small field to the road in Heathcote. A short distance to the right, past a farm on the left, is a signpost to Friden. Cross the field obliquely right to a stile and here take a sighting for the route ahead. The raised embankment of the Tissington Trail can be seen, as can a bridge that carries it. Away to the right are two gates facing each other across the track. Aim for this point going over several stiles en route. Having gained The Trail, turn right for an easy walk back to the car park in Alsop with fine views along the Dove Valley to Axe Edge.

REFRESHMENTS:
The Waterloo Inn, Biggin (tel no: 0298 284).
There is a shop/café in Milldale.

Walk 16 **SHARDLOW** 3m (5km)

Maps: OS Sheets Landranger 129; Pathfinder SK 43/53.

A walk to one of the best inland ports in England.

Start: The public car park in Shardlow.

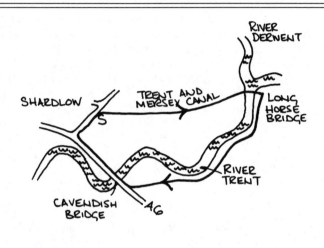

Go right out of the car park and along Wilne Lane to a bridge over the Trent and Mersey canal. Do not go over, but turn left and go down to the canal towpath. Turn right and follow the towpath for almost a mile to the junction of the Trent and Derwent. Cross Long Horse Bridge over the Trent and turn right. Follow the river bank for about $^3/_4$ mile over two stiles to where the river turns sharp right. Here go straight ahead across a field to a stile and footpath sign. Go over the stile to the A6 and turn right over Cavendish Bridge, following the road back into **Shardlow**. Go past Wilne Lane and the Navigation Inn to reach the canal again and follow the towpath right, back to the first bridge. Go up to Wilne Lane and turn right back to the car park.

POINTS OF INTEREST:
Shardlow – This fine port was the start of the 92 mile long Trent and Mersey Canal. The village is well worth exploring. There is a plaque of charges near Cavendish Bridge and Clock Warehouse has a canal museum.

REFRESHMENTS:
The Navigation Inn, Shardlow (tel no: 0332 571242).

Walk 17   **DRUM HILL AND MORLEY**   3m (5km)
Maps: OS Sheets Landranger 119; Pathfinder SK 24/34.
A pleasant walk through fields and woods.
Start: At 381417, a lay-by on Morley Lane.

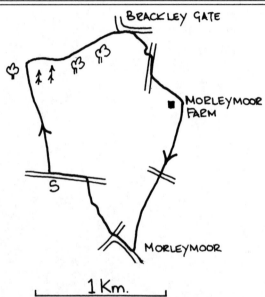

1 Km.

Follow the footpath signed from the lay-by through several fields to a wood. The walk goes straight on down through the wood, though you may wish first to explore the woodland paths. At the bottom of the wood go over a stile and turn right on the track. After a short way, after two gates, the track narrows and goes uphill, past a turning to the right up to houses at Brackley Gate. Go past the houses, now on a metalled road, turn right at Sandy Lane and almost immediately right again on a path signed between two houses. Go between gardens a short way to reach a wire fence. Turn right, then left along a fence to the road. Turn right on the road then left on a path just beyond the bus shelter. Go over a field towards Morleymoor Farm, around the left-hand side of a barn, then to the right along a fence to a stile. Here you cross a farm road and continue along a track, parallel to 'Quarry Road' marked on the map. The track leads to a road where you cross straight over on to a footpath, which goes along the edge of a Derbyshire

Wildlife Trust **Nature Reserve**. The path continues through fields to the eastern side of the small settlement of Morleymoor. When the path comes close to the road, go through a gate on the right. Turn right on the road, passing the chapel and almshouses on Moor Road the Roman road, called **Ryknild Street**.

Cross straight over to a path opposite which goes over two fields, left along a hedge then right over a stile in the corner by the wall bordering a golf course. This leads you back to Morley Lane, where you turn left back to your starting point.

POINTS OF INTEREST:

Nature Reserve – Known as Morley Brickyards and consisting of woodland and flooded clay pits. May be entered from the road you have just crossed.

Ryknild Street – Built for the Roman advance northwards from Cirencester to Chesterfield and, later, on to Templeborough.

Maps: OS Sheets Landranger 129; Pathfinder SK 43/53.
A short walk through a fine country park.
Start: The car park in Elvaston Castle Country Park.

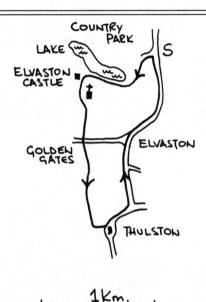

From the car park follow the path to the lake and continue to **Elvaston Castle**. Go left to the church and on through the topiary gardens to reach the Golden Gates, now painted an inglorious shade of blue. Ahead and left now is a kissing gate. Go through and follow a path across a field to reach another kissing gate. Go through to reach yet another beyond which the path goes left to reach Brook Road. Follow this to Thulston, where the Harrington Arms Inn is to the left. To return either retrace your steps or follow the road beyond the Inn, going left for Elvaston village. Bear right in the village on a road back to the car park.

POINTS OF INTEREST:
Elvaston Castle – The Castle was rebuilt in the early 19th century in Gothic style by the Stanhope family. The Stanhopes became the Earls of Harrington and the church has several monuments to them. The Golden Gates came from a Royal Palace in Madrid. In 1969 the estate was taken over by Derbyshire County Council and turned into a Country Park.

REFRESHMENTS:
The Harrington Arms, Thulston (tel no: 0332 571798).

Walk 19   **CROMFORD CANAL AND CRICH CHASE**   4m (6.5km)
Maps: OS Sheets Landranger 119; Outdoor Leisure 24.
A varied walk of woodland, open hilltop and canal towpath.
Start: At 339533, the car park between Whatstandwell and
Ambergate.

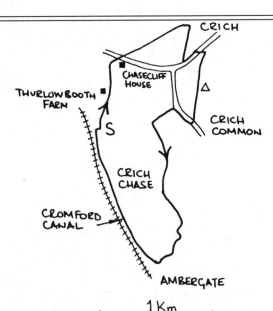

Take the main track northwards out of the car park, keeping to the lower path. Continue
past a sign 'Private Road Thurlowbooth Farm Only': this refers only to traffic, and a
public Right of Way leads past the house and over a stile. A short way further on, just
past a private garage, turn right up a path which goes steeply up by a wall, the boundary
wall of the grounds of Chase Cliff. Emerging on to a road, turn right and then left on
a footpath by Chase Cliff Farm. The path follows a wall through two fields and then
through a long narrow field to a stile. Go over to a road through a small housing estate
on the edge of Crich. Go down the road to a crossroads where you turn right on to a
footpath over a stile. Keep straight ahead through fields to a road (B5035) where you
turn back left until you see a lay-by and footpath on the right. From the road you have
views over the Derwent valley to Alport Heights (see Walk 31) and to **Crich Stand**.

Take the footpath across a field to a stile and kissing gate. Do not go through but turn right along the wall over a hilltop known as The Tors. Here there are views southeast as far as the Trent power stations on a clear day. The way goes over several stiles and gradually downhill to a road via a stile and steps near the bottom on your left. Turn right to a bend where you take a footpath on the left, which leads through two fields to the top of Crich Chase, an area of old woodland on a steep drop to the **Cromford Canal**.

At the Chase, the path turns sharp left and makes a gradual descent through woods. Keep to the main path. After about 1 mile, where there appears to be a choice of paths, keep first to a left-hand fork then straight over a forest ride. Take the higher path at another fork to avoid mud, after which you emerge over a stile into a small field. Turn diagonally right across the field and go out through a gate. Go over the canal bridge. Now go right, down on to the canal towpath which you follow for about 1 mile till you come to a bridge, over which, to the right, you will find the car park. This stretch of the canal is a nature reserve.

POINTS OF INTEREST:

Crich Stand – A war memorial to the Sherwood Foresters Regiment 950ft above sea level. The tower is open daily and worth a visit for the views. Below in the old quarry is the National Tramway Museum, also well worth a visit.

Cromford Canal – Used for the transport of lead ore and textiles and linked products from 1793 to 1944. The stretch between Ambergate and Whatstandwell is preserved as a nature reserve by Derbyshire County Council, the Cromford Canal Society and the Derbyshire Wildlife Trust.

REFRESHMENTS:

Nowhere en route unless a detour is made into Crich village.

Walk 20   DALE TO LOCKO PARK   4¹/₂m (7km)

Maps: OS Sheets Landranger 129; Pathfinder SK 43/53.

A walk linking an interesting village and a fine park.

Start: At 438390, in the village of Dale.

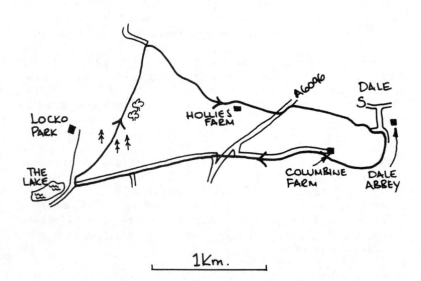

Go south through the village past Abbey House and the last ruin of the Abbey itself. Go on to the church and take the track on its right to a gate and Public Bridleway signed 'Dunnshill'. Through the gate the path to the left leads to the Hermit's Cave, but we go ahead on a track that goes over a stile and through a gate into open country. The Dale Hills are to your left. The track reaches a gate and stile before Columbine Farm. Go round this to the left and on to the farm track. Follow this to where it goes sharp right. Go ahead here on a track to a road. Cross to a track with a Public Bridleway signed 'Locko Park'. Follow this track into **Locko Park**.

Go through a gate and follow the now metalled track to The Lake. Go right at a T-junction near the lake, and right again through a kissing gate. Go up a path towards a wood. The house of Locko Park is to the left here. Go over a ladder stile into the wood and at the other side go through a kissing gate into a field. Keep the fence on your right and cross a footbridge. Continue with a wood on the right to a stile at the wood's end. Now keep a fence on your right to reach a stile. Go over and follow a fence on your left to reach a track from Hill Farm at a gate and stile. Turn right, following the hedge, through two gates on to a hedged track. Walk along this to a gate and through it to a stile. The track goes left to Hollies Farm. Go around left of the farm and down the farm lane to the A6096. Cross the road and go left a few yards later to a gate and footpath sign. Go through and follow a grass track across a field to a gate. Pass through and down to another gate. Go through and cross a field to arrow-shaped end and a stile. Cross over on to a track and follow it to a stile. Go over and down the path, to the left to a road. Go along the road into **Dale** and the start of the walk.

POINTS OF INTEREST:
Locko Park – The house dates from the mid-18th century but the chapel is earlier. There are major riding events here each year.
Dale – Little now remains of Dale Abbey, just a 40-foot high window arch standing in a field. The stained glass windows from this were saved and are in Morley church, 4 miles away.

REFRESHMENTS:
The Carpenters Arms, Dale (tel no: 0602 325 277).

Walk 21 **SWARKESTONE** 4$\frac{1}{2}$m (7km)

Maps: OS Sheets Landranger 128; Pathfinder SK 22/32.

A gentle walk along river and canal.

Start: At 347286, the lay-by on the Barrow-on-Trent by-pass.

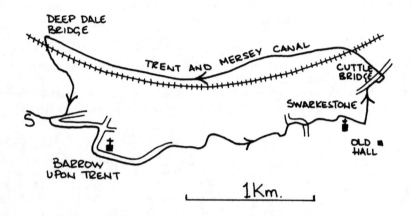

Cross the by-pass and turn right into **Barrow** village, an attractive mix of old and new houses and cottages. At the village cross roads turn right down Church Lane noting the old Pinfold on the right just before reaching St Wilfred's Church. Walk past the church to the 15th-century Crow Trees Cottage. Take the path between the cottage garden and the River Trent and, after crossing a footbridge, continue along the river into a field. Several fields have been made into one large field here and the original path line shown on the OS map cannot be followed. Instead, turn left and walk along two sides of the field to reach a rough farm track. Turn right along it and follow the fence round to a small building by the river. Go left along the river bank a little way and then diagonally left to a rough path right of the two houses. Cross a stile at the top of the path to enter Swarkestone village street. Turn right to the T-junction and Crewe and Harpur Inn, an 18th-century coaching inn (hence the large stable block). To the right is **Swarkestone**

Bridge. Take the path to the left of the small wooden fence and follow it through to the church. To the right is **Swarkestone Bridge Causeway.** On reaching the church, go left along the road leaving it at the bend to go right to a gate and stile by the wall corner. Go over and follow the line of the wall across a field to meet the farm drive adjacent to a converted barn. The barn and the long garden wall are all that remain of **Swarkestone Hall.**

Walk along the farm road to the left, passing by an unusual Jacobean-style building which was either a summer house for the Hall or possibly a grandstand for watching bull-baiting or bowls. At a T-junction with the main road, turn right towards Cuttle Bridge and descend through a gap in the railings to the towpath of the Trent and Mersey canal, the work of James Brindley. Pass under the bridge and after $1/_4$ mile reach Swarkestone Lock. Just beyond is a junction with Derby canal, long since defunct. Continue along the well-kept towpath, with Willington Power Station ahead to reach Bridge No 17 (Deep Dale) shortly after passing a milestone reading 'Shardlow 7 miles – Preston Brook 85 miles'. Ascend from the towpath to a farm track which is followed left over the railway bridge to a pair of gates. Pass through the left-hand gate, and another across the field, before veering right to cross a bridge over a stream. At the far end of the next field is a gate to the by-pass. Turn right to reach the starting point of the walk.

POINTS OF INTEREST:

Barrow – The old Pinfold was once used for the impounding of stray livestock until claimed by their owners. Sir Nicholas Pevsner believed the church's most remarkable feature was the north arcade with its mid-13th century piers.

Swarkestone Bridge – The southernmost point reached by Bonnie Prince Charlie in 1745.

Swarkestone Bridge Causeway – Reference has been found to this from as far back as 1204. Built, according to legend, by sisters in memory of boyfriends drowned while trying to cross the flooded plain. It was more likely built by Repton Priory.

Swarkestone Hall – Demolished after the Civil War to punish its Royalist owner, Sir John Harpur.

REFRESHMENTS:
The Crewe and Harpur Inn, Swarkestone (tel no: 0332 700641).

Walk 22 CRICH AND SOUTH WINGFIELD MANOR 4¹/₄m (7km)

Maps: OS Sheets Landranger 119; Pathfinder SK 25/35.

*A walk mainly through fields with gentle ascents and visiting an
interesting ruin.*

Start: At 350542, Crich market place.

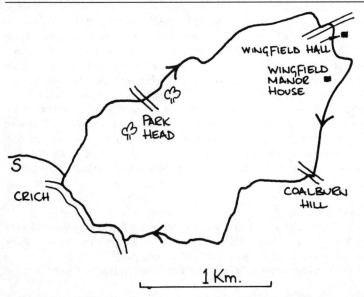

Leave Crich by School Lane. Follow the path with a high wire fence to the left. After
a stile cross left to another stile at a gateway. Cross the field, skirting a quarry, to cross
its access road to a brook. Go over this and follow the field hedge to a stile at the junction
of hedges. Continue through fields to the road at Park Head. Use the stile near two trees
opposite and cross fields to two stiles in close succession. Turn left for 20 yards up a
lane to a squeeze stile on the right. Go through and keep left of the farm. At a gate at
a power line pole go directly ahead to a stile in a hedge. Turn right and in the second
field turn left to a 'squeeze' in a hedge. The ruins of **South Wingfield Manor** can be
seen to the right.

Cross the next field and part way down the next field cross a stile in the hedge on
the left and follow the hedges down to a gate. Left over the gate is a stile and a brook.

Go over and bear right to a stile in the corner and continue to a road. Turn left up the hill to a drive on the right leading in the direction of the Manor. Follow this to take a track to the right at the top of a rise. Where the wall ends go forward to pass the entrance to the manor. Pass Manor Farm and continue along the track until a path leaves left through a gateway. This path is followed alongside hedges until it drops down to join a minor road below Coalburn Hill. Turn right and almost immediately left at a footpath sign beside a gate. In the field turn half right to a gate and stile. The path passes to the right of the building ahead. Cross a double stile and leave the field by a gap in the bottom corner (this section can be quite muddy) to cross a brook and reach a stile at a wooden gate. Follow the track as it turns first right and then left into the next field. Keep parallel with the wall and at the top of the field turn right between walls to trees at their end. Follow the path to leave the trees and cross a field into a further wood, mainly of holly trees. The path ahead is clear, but just before leaving the wood leave it to the left to emerge from the wood over a stile near a farm. Turn left downhill to a gate and continue down to join a road. Turn right and follow the road past dwellings in a converted hat factory to take the road to the right almost on the edge of Crich village. This joins the outward route at a stile on the left. Retrace your steps along the high fence via School Lane into Crich and the starting point of the walk.

POINTS OF INTEREST:
South Wingfield Manor – Not yet open to the public but work is in hand. Close to the National Tramway Museum (077 385 2565) and to the viewpoint of the Crich Stand.

REFRESHMENTS:
Available in Crich and at the Tramway Museum.

DETHICK AND LEA HURST 5m (8km)

Maps: OS Sheets Landranger 119; Outdoor Leisure 24.

A fine walk through woods and rhododendrons.

Start: At 328581, in the village of Dethick.

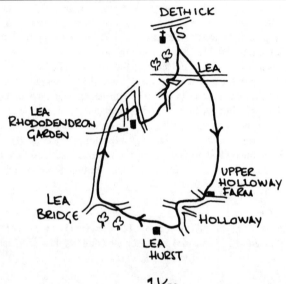

Go down to the church and along a path to its left going across a field to a stile and on to a second stile. Walk across the middle of the next field to a stile into woodland. Follow a path through this and down to a footbridge. Cross over and climb to a road. Go right to Lea Chapel. Just beyond, take a lane to the left signed 'Upper Holloway and Wakebridge'. Where the lane ends go right on a signed footpath across a field to two stiles. Go over and on to another. Go over and down a hollow. Turn right and walk along this, passing a footpath signed 'Upper Holloway'. This footpath becomes a walled track. Follow it to where it turns sharp right and then go ahead to a stile. Go over and cross the field to a stile. Go over and cross a field to another stile, and a footpath sign. Go over, and down the wall to Upper Holloway Farm. Go round the right-hand side of the farm and over several stiles on to a road. Turn left, then right and down the lane to Holloway. Turn left then right along Bracken Lane. After about 100 yards, where the road goes left in front of a cottage on the right, go right over a stile and along a path to a field corner. Do not go over the stile, left, but go right along the field edge to cross the drive of **Lea Hurst**.

Follow a path round the garden wall to a stile. Cross over and down to another stile. Beyond this the path bears right to a kissing gate on to Mill Lane. Go left and down to Lea Bridge.

At Lea Bridge go right along Lea Road for $\frac{1}{2}$ mile to a footpath sign to the right. Take this path to reach a road. Go over and take another path to another road. Turn right past the entrance to **Lea Rhododendron Gardens**.

About 100 yards beyond the entrance is a footpath sign at a kissing gate to the left. Pass through and follow the path around playing fields to a lane. Turn left. Go over at a crossroads and on to a T-junction. Lea Post Office is to the right here. Cross the road to reach a gate. Go through and follow the path to a gate. Go through and turn right. You soon go left at a footpath sign and down steps to a footbridge. Go over and up through trees to a stile. Go over and left around a field to another. Now reverse the outward route to **Dethick**.

POINTS OF INTEREST:

Lea Hurst – Florence Nightingale, 'The Lady with the Lamp', was born in Florence but lived here after her Crimea exploits. The house was built in the 17th century but was enlarged by Florence's father. His date stamp (N1825) is above the main door. Florence died on 13 August 1910. Today, fittingly, Lea Hurst is a home for elderly folk.

Lea Rhododendron Gardens – These magnificent rhododendron and azalea gardens were laid out by J B Marsden-Smedley and are open to the public from Easter to mid-June.

Dethick – This beautiful village is grouped around 'The church in the farmyard'. The church tower was built by Sir Anthony Babington who was executed for his attempts to rescue Mary, Queen of Scots.

REFRESHMENTS:

The Jug and Glass Inn, Lea (tel no: 0629 534232).
The Yew Tree Inn, Holloway (tel no: 0629 524355).

Walk 24　　TICKNALL AND CALKE ABBEY　　5m (8km)

Maps: OS Sheets Landranger 128; Pathfinder SK 22/32.

An easy walk through wooded countryside and visiting Calke Abbey and Park.

Start: At 349241, an unofficial car park in Ticknall.

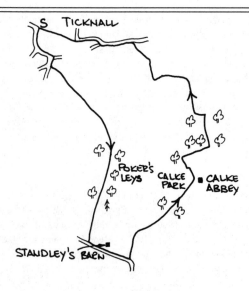

From the car park entrance turn left to a road junction then left again and first right (Ashby Road). Just past the Staff of Life Inn, a footpath sign by a house points the way over a stile into a field. The path is clear to see, first alongside a brick wall and then across the field to a stile in the corner. Continue on a straight line across three more fields and stiles to enter a fourth with the tree-lined drive to Calke Abbey coming in from the left. The path line is along a mound until, nearing Middle Lodge, it veers right to a stile by a gate. Cross the stile and follow a path, first along the wall of Calke Park, and then the edge of Poker's Leys (wood) to reach a gate at the end of the trees. Go through, cross the field on a line just left of a telegraph pole on the right to exit on to a road via a small wooden gate. Go left to a sharp right-hand bend and a rough track on the left. Follow this to a white double gate and Calke Park beyond. Continue straight down the drive with a magnificent view ahead of **Calke Abbey**. Beyond are the waters of Staunton Harold Reservoir.

The OS map shows a public footpath but there is no longer a Right of Way. However an alternative route has been provided. Turn left along the front of the Abbey stable block into the car park. Leave this via a wooden gate in the left wall. Follow the wall right on a path leading to a newly constructed series of steps down to a path along by Mere Pond, a good spot for water birds. At the end of the water turn left and, after passing through a gate, ascend the hillside along by a high wire fence which is the boundary of a deer park. On reaching the top go left along the wall to an inset gate. Go through, turn left and pass into the next field via a hedge gap. Follow a path around two sides of the field to a stile in the far corner. Cross over the stile, a farm road and another stile, keep ahead along the left boundary and walk round the corner to a gap, ignoring the footpath sign pointing right. Go through the gap, turn right on to a track by the wood continuing through trees, with flooded pits on either side. Clay was extracted from these pits in the 19th century. A little further on the track meets the road through the village of **Ticknall**.

Walk along the road to the left, under the arch (a bridge that once carried the light railway known as the **Ticknall Tramway**) to a grassed area opposite the entrance to Calke Abbey. Go between the two posts in the corner on to a side street and walk to the road junction. Opposite is a dual signpost, the right-hand one showing the walk direction across the field to a corner stile. Cross the stile, turning left along the boundary to cross another stile in the corner. Turn left through a gate to reach the road and, in a few yards, the car park and the start of the walk.

POINTS OF INTEREST:
Calke Abbey – Built in 1703 as the home of the Harpur-Crewe family it is the least known of Derbyshire's great houses. Taken over by the National Trust in 1985 who discovered that many of the Abbey's 90 rooms had remained untouched for upwards of 150 years. Nothing remains of the original Augustinian Abbey on the site.
Ticknall – Once a thriving brick and pottery village. The church was built in 1842.
Ticknall Tramway – Was used by horse-drawn wagons to carry lime and clay from the now flooded pits and the products of the brick and pottery works to the canal at Ashby-de-la-Zouch.

REFRESHMENTS:
The Staff of Life, Ticknall (tel no: 0332 862479).

Walk 25   KIRK IRETON TO MILLERS GREEN   6m (11.5km)

Maps: OS Sheets Landranger 119; Pathfinder SK 25/35.

A stiff road walk, but surrounded by superb views.

Start: At 265501, near the Barley Mow, Kirk Ireton.

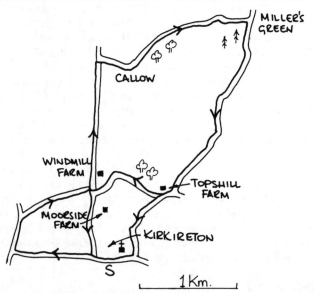

From the Barley Mow follow the Callow Hopton road for about 100 yards and then turn left along a narrow road for about $^1/_2$ mile until you come to a T-junction. Go right . Almost immediately fine views towards Alport radio masts on the right and the hills of the southern Peak District can be enjoyed.

Continue for $^3/_4$ mile along this road until you reach a crossroads at Moorside. Here the route goes left towards Callow. After a further $^3/_4$ mile go right and continue along the road downhill to Miller's Green. From this point the market town of Wirksworth can be seen on the left and is, in fact, only about 1 mile from Miller's Green should you wish to deviate from the route.

At the junction in Miller's Green turn right up a mile-long hill to Topshill. You will pass Alton Manor on the left. From the crossroads at Topshill there are two routes back to the start and your choice will depend upon how you feel after the mile-long hill.

There is a direct route which continues over the crossroads for $^1/_2$ mile back to **Kirk Ireton** or you can turn right towards Moorside and Windmill Farm. At the next crossroads the route goes left and back to the Barley Mow.

POINTS OF INTEREST:
Kirk Ireton – Situated in the beautiful rolling hills of central Derbyshire. Most of the cottages are constructed from the limestone mined at nearby quarries. The surrounding villages are equally attractive and a deviation into Wirksworth is worthwhile to see the craft village set back off the main road. Here local people can be found pursuing the crafts of yesteryear.

REFRESHMENTS:
The Barley Mow, Kirk Ireton (tel no: 0335 70306).
There are an assortment of pubs and cafés in Wirksworth.

Walk 26　　**TICKNALL AND FOREMARK**　　6m (9.5km)

Maps: OS Sheets Landranger 128; Pathfinder SK 22/32.

A pleasant easy walk along clear footpaths and bridleways.

Start: At 349241, the unofficial car park, Ticknall.

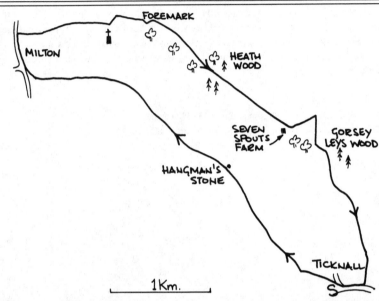

Leave the car park by the entrance and turn right. Go through a gate at a sharp bend in the road. Turn sharp left to follow a path along the field boundary. Go through several fields to a gate. Go through and follow the right-hand boundary on a bridle path. After passing through a gate and a plantation of trees, cross a stile into a field. There is no path line visible, so walk straight ahead up the field. A stile comes into view: cross it and take a track leading to a minor road by Saw Mill Cottage. Follow the road as it swings right into Milton's only street. Walk along the right side of the street, past the Swan Inn to reach a telephone box. A few yards further on a footpath sign points the way along a short path by the side of a house. Cross a stile and follow the short path to a footbridge. The next short section may be very muddy. If so follow the wire fence on the left. Go through a gate into a field. Ascend to the far left corner to a gate. Pass through and follow a line parallel to the right boundary across two fields and fence stiles to meet a rough road with **Foremark Church** to the right. Turn left along the road and shortly turn right up another road, through trees, into the grounds of **Foremark Hall**. A sign says 'Private Road' but it is a public footpath.

Walk along the road with the Hall away to the right, passing the end of the lake on your left, to follow another road as it curves left between school buildings to arrive at the village street with a telephone box immediately opposite. Go along the wide track to the right of the box, ascending through historic **Heath Wood** to meet a minor road. Donnington Power Station can be seen ahead and left.

Cross the road and follow the track to Seven Spouts Farm, so called after the seven springs nearby. Where the track swings left, keep ahead over a stile. Continue along another track and through a fence gap to the field beyond. Keep to the track across the field to the boundary wall, turning right to follow it until a footpath sign points the way over a stile between two gates. The path descends a slight slope before turning right at the bottom on a clear line across the field to Gorsey Leys Wood. Follow the distinct path through the trees to a gate. Go through into a field and left across it to another gate. Go through and turn right along the boundary. From here the path is well-defined across further fields to a gate and a grassed area opposite the entrance to Calke Abbey (see Walk 24). Turn sharply right to pass between two posts by a gate on to the village side street. Walk along the street, past the Methodist Chapel (1815) to a road junction with a dual footpath sign on the far side. Follow the right-hand direction across the field passing, on the left, the church and its predecessor's remains. Cross the stile in the field corner, turning left along the boundary to another corner stile. Go over this and turn left through a gate to the road and start point.

POINTS OF INTEREST:
Foremark Church – Built by Sir Francis Burdell in 1662 in the Gothic style.
Foremark Hall – Built in 1760 in Palladian style by Sir Robert Burdell. Now the hall and the newer building are a preparatory school for Repton School.
Heath Wood – Contains a Danish barrow cemetery, estimated from exhumations to be of the late 9th century.

REFRESHMENTS:
The Swan Inn, Milton (tel no: 0283 703188).
The Staff of Life, Ticknall (tel no: 0332 862479).

Walk 27 **DALBURY** 6$\frac{1}{2}$m (10km)

Maps: OS Sheets Landranger 128; Pathfinder SK 23/33.

A walk in a really quiet area of Derbyshire.

Start: The church in Dalbury.

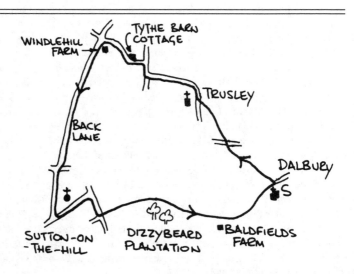

From the church go to the end of the metalled lane to a gate. Go through and turn right to another gate. Go through and left along the edge of a field to reach a gap at the top left-hand corner of the next field. Bear right to a stile. Bear left to reach a footbridge, cross and go right to a farm. Cross the road ahead to a gate. Go through and across the field to the left-hand corner and a stile. Go over and on to two more stiles. Now bear left to reach steps and a stile. Go right through Trusley village. At a road junction about $\frac{1}{2}$ mile further on, turn right and then left along a lane past Tythe Barn Cottage to a road junction near Windlehill Farm. Go left for about a mile to a T-junction. Go right, then left by the chapel. At the next T-junction go left past the church of Sutton-on-the-Hill, well removed from the village. Go right at the next T-junction and at a crossroads go left through a gate on a path signed 'Dalbury – 2 miles'. Follow the hedge, right, to another gate. Go through and around the end of Dizzybeard Plantation. Go across a field to a gate and on through two more towards Baldfields Farm. Keep left of the farm through a field to a gate. Go through and left towards **Dalbury Church** to reach a gate and several footbridges. Go over and on to a stile. Go over to the church and your start point.

POINTS OF INTEREST:
Dalbury Church – The church has the oldest piece of stained glass in Derbyshire, a figure of St Michael dated to around 1200.

Walk 28   STAUNTON HAROLD RESERVOIR $6\frac{1}{2}$m (10km)
Maps: OS Sheets Landranger 128; Pathfinder SK 22/32.
A walk with wide views over the River Trent valley.
Start: At 377245, Staunton Harold Reservoir car park.

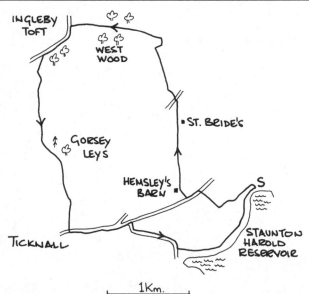

Cross the stile adjacent to the observation tower (once a windmill) and turn left on a
clear path to the far corner of the field and a stile. Go over and at the footpath sign turn
right and walk along a drive to its junction with the Ticknall to Melbourne road. Turn
left along the road for 100 yards and then right along a farm track which passes
Hemsley's Barn and St Bride's, once a monastic grange. Continue along the track, with
views of the Trent valley and Donnington Power Station, to its junction with the
Ticknall to Stanton road. Cross over and follow the signed bridleway on a slight zig-
zag across the fields to meet a private road. Here are further fine views, with the River
Trent and Willington Power Station in the foreground and the suburbs of Derby
beyond. Walk left along the road which, after passing a private house, becomes a track
alongside West Wood before ascending to a minor road opposite **Ingleby Toft,** a red-
brick Georgian house.

Go left along the minor road, leaving it at a sharp bend to pass through a gate. Follow a path alongside Robin Wood. On reaching a small wooden gate and a footpath signpost on your right, turn along a path through the trees to cross a stile. Ascend the path ahead. At the top, go over a stile to pass a derelict cottage, which from its layout was much more than a labourer's dwelling. One wonders who built in this remote spot and what events caused its abandonment. Continue alongside the wooded valley. Go over a fence stile at its end and across the field beyond to pass through a gate into a wood. Follow the clear path through the trees and go through a gate at the far side into a field. Cross to the far left corner. Pass through the gate and turn right along a well-trodden path by the field boundary. The way ahead is clearly seen across several fields to exit via a gate into Ticknall opposite the entrance to Calke Abbey (see Walk 24). Walk along the road to the left, passing under the arch of a bridge which carried the long defunct Ticknall Tramway (see Walk 24) to a road junction. Turn right up the Melbourne road to a minor road opposite a pair of cottages (nos 17 and 19). Walk down this road. Near its end turn along the road skirting the reservoir and follow it back to the car park and the start of the walk.

POINTS OF INTEREST:
Ingleby Toft – This delightful name is Danish and means 'the farm at the place of the English'.

REFRESHMENTS:
The Melbourne Arms, Melbourne (tel no: 0332 863990).

Walks 29 & 30 HIGH PEAK JUNCTION AND RIBER 7m (11km)

Maps: OS Sheets Landranger 119; Pathfinder SK 25/35.

An interesting and varied walk with one steepish climb.

Start: At 315561, the High Peak Junction car park at Lea Bridge.

Leave the car park going over the Derwent to **High Peak Junction** on the Cromford canal. Turn left along the towpath following the sign 'Ambergate'. Pass an engine house and cross the river and railway by aqueducts to reach a point where the canal enters a tunnel. Leave the towpath here and go up the rise to a gate, left. In the field beyond the path is marked with white posts. Follow the path to a gate and a stile to a road which is followed uphill, left, to a road. Turn left and then right after 20 yards up 'The Hollow'. Take the first road left at the top (Long Lane). Pass farm buildings, take the stile on the right and cross to a gate. Go through and turn half-left. Follow the well-marked path to a gate and stile and cross to a tall dead tree at a wall corner. Bear left to a stile into a grassy lane. Follow the lane, keeping left at a white gate post to a stile, left, just beyond the Wakebridge signpost. Cross the stile to two more near a large tree. Go half-right to a stile on to a track. Follow this for some yards to an opening, right, between houses leading to the main road through Lea village. Over the road a footpath leads through trees. Take this to cross a brook and, keeping right at a fork in the path, enter fields at a stile. Follow the edge of the fields, left, joining a path from the left and continue to the church at Dethick. Pass to the right of the church and turn left to cross a minor road to a step stile in the wall at a signpost. Follow the line of the wall across several fields. Leave it as it swings left and cross to a white gate. Beyond, turn right to a road and then left to a road junction. Turn left for 250 yards to a stile on the right where a hedge begins. Cross the stile and follow the wall in the direction of **Riber Castle**.

The path joins a broad green way and passes a house before joining a surfaced farm road. Follow this to a stile in the wall, left. Go over to a road in Riber village. Turn left, passing Riber Farm Shop, and go left at the road junction to a stile at the telephone pole on the right. Cross to a further stile and follow the edge of the fields towards the buildings of Hearthstone. Pass them on the right to join a road. Turn left. Turn right up a walled track at a cattle grid and follow it over Bilberry Knoll and, as the track begins to descend steeply (*), take the path to the left to pass left of a roofless building to a stile by a silver birch. Follow the path down over a wall stile. Bear right across the top edge of a boggy area to cross fields to a stile into a wood. Follow a path to a stile. Turn half-right to a stile at the top of a field and follow the path left along the top of the wood and then right down through the trees. The path finally reaches a low broken wall which is crossed. Drop steeply down to join a heavily-used path which leads left to the main road. Turn right along the road to reach the start.

(*) For an alternative route follow the path downhill to reach a gate into fields. After a gate with a stile the track continues between walls and swings right through another gate to join a track from a farm leading left downhill. As the track bends sharply right follow a path leading left to pass along the edge of a garden and enter woods. Follow the path to the Cromford-Crich road. Turn right along the road to reach the start.

POINTS OF INTEREST:

High Peak Junction – This is where Cromford and High Peak Railway transferred goods from rail to barge. There is an information centre.

Riber Castle – Built in the 19th century by a local textile magnate. It is now a shell. There is a wildlife park on the site.

REFRESHMENTS:

The Hayloft Tearoom, Riber Hall Farm.

Walks 31 & 32 AROUND ALPORT HEIGHT 7¹/₂m (12km)

Maps: OS Sheets Landranger 119; Outdoor Leisure 24.

An easy walk on paths and unspoilt country lanes and including 1 mile of wood and parkland.

Start: At 304516, Alport Height car park.

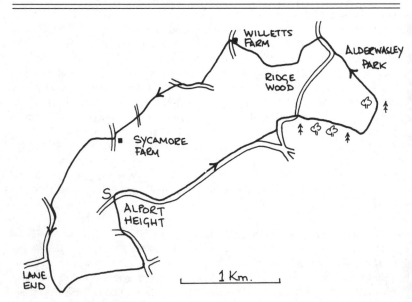

Leave the car park, turn right at the crossroads and go down the lane for just over 1 mile. Where it turns right by the entrance to 'Clearsprings' go over a stile and across three fields to a road. Turn left, then shortly right to Higg Lane. A short way down on the right, by a lay-by, turn into the wood. Take either path, sharp left or next left, which emerge from the wood at a gate. Go through, along a wall, then between walls and through the next gate. The path through Alderwasley Park is now easy to follow. It bears left once out of the woodland and continues down to the road. Turn right, then left on a track into Kennel Wood. The path turns left past a house, and forks right at a drive to another house. Continue up the track to Ridgewood Cottage and go through the stile on the right. Take the path by the wall, turn right when it joins a track and go over a stile on the left opposite 'The Little House' at Little Hayes Farm. At a road turn

70

right, then left on a footpath opposite Willetts Farm. This path goes up by the wall through four fields. Just before a road you meet a fence. Turn right here on to the road. Turn right. Just before a road junction you will see a stile into a conifer plantation. Go through the plantation diagonally (not left by the wall) to a stile and footpath sign at the wall on the other side. The path continues in the direction of the sign over two stiles and then follows the wall on your right over two more stiles on to a lane. Continue straight opposite through two fields, past a cottage to a stile in the left-hand corner of the field then on past Sycamore Farm to the road via a stile in the left-hand corner of the field.

Turn left (not sharp left) on the road then almost immediately right on a track just before Broadgates Farm. (The walk may be terminated after Broadgates by continuing on up that lane to Alport Height omitting about $2^1/_2$ miles.) Go over the cattle grid and keep straight ahead between two walls to a stile. Go straight on by the wall to a stile near a gate around the bend to the left. Do not follow the farm track, but make for the left-hand corner of the wood you see to your right. There climb over the wall by a step stile bear left round the top of the field to the next stile, diagonally right to the next and on in a straight line to another. You cannot go over this one, so turn right to another among trees and another by a gate opposite. Continue downhill past the upper side of a small wood. When you see a gate ahead go past it to the right, to a stile on to a road. Turn left up the lane to Lane End, ignoring a left-hand turning. At Lane End, where the road bends to the right, take a track on the left to Lane End Farm. Go over a gate and continue over another gate (this is a Right of Way, but it is neither marked nor well used). Cross the field, then turn left along the boundary fence to a stile. After the next field bear right down to a stream. Cross this and go on up hill by the wall to a stile at the top. Continue on to the next stile then on to the road. Turn left to the hamlet of Spout where you turn right up Alport Lane back to **Alport Height.**

POINTS OF INTEREST:
Alport Height – The name Alport (there are three in Derbyshire, marking the line of the Old Portway) derives from the Saxon, 'Al' from Ald (Old) and 'Port' a pathway. The Saxons used it to differentiate the old route from their own. The hill is 1,034 ft high and is topped by aerials of the Derbyshire County Police Radio Station.

Walk 33   QUARNDON AND KEDLESTON   7¹/₂m (12km)

Maps: OS Sheets Landranger 119 & 128; Pathfinder SK 23/33 & SK 24/34.

An easy walk following mainly well-defined tracks.

Start: At 334410, in the village of Quarndon.

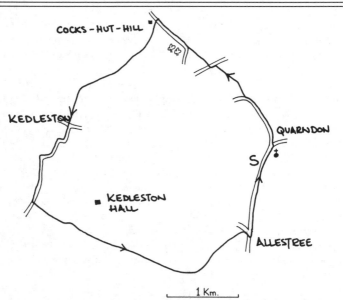

1 Km.

Starting from the lay-by opposite the delicatessen walk north past the church of St Pauls. Turn left on to the road signposted 'Windley'. Just after a sharp left-hand bend there is a stile and gate next to a cottage on the right. Go over and cross fields following the yellow arrow markings. At the second hedge go diagonally left across the field to a road. Turn left and follow the road for 100 yards. Take the footpath on the right. Cross the field keeping the hedge on the left. At the end of the field cross the stile on the left and follow the field ahead to a stile. Join the lane and go right. Follow the road for nearly ¹/₂ mile until Cockshutt Farmyard is seen on the left. Go through the farmyard and follow the track across the fields keeping the farm behind you. Go through the gate and cross the field to a gate in the opposite left-hand corner. Cross the next field following the left-hand hedge to a double stile. Cross the field to the double gate opposite at the edge of the woods. Follow the fence on the left and as it turns left continue down the field, bearing slightly left to the bottom left-hand corner. Go through the ford and turn left. Follow the woods round, and cross the hedge ahead at the mid-way point. Carry on towards the gabled cottage to meet the main road. Go over the road and down the road opposite signposted **Kedleston Hall.**

Pass the Hall and follow the road round a sharp right-hand bend. Turn left on to the road for Kirk Langley. Continue for $^3/_4$ mile until a bridleway goes left opposite Priestwood Farm. Follow the bridleway for $2^1/_4$ miles, passing Upper Vickarwood Farm until the main road is reached. Turn right and at T-junction turn left towards Quarndon. On reaching the village the Joiners Arms pub is on the right-hand side. The lay-by is a few hundred yards further on.

POINTS OF INTEREST:
Kedleston Hall – Pre-17th-century stately home. Open to the public 25 March – end of October. Park and gardens open 11am – 6pm. Restaurant open 12 noon – 5pm. Hall and shop open 1pm – 5.30pm.

REFRESHMENTS:
The Joiners Arms, Quarndon.

Walk 34   AROUND MILFORD   12m (19km)

Maps: OS Sheets Landranger 119; Outdoor Leisure 24.

Magnificent views across East Derbyshire.

Start: At 351450, the bridge over the River Derwent, Milford.

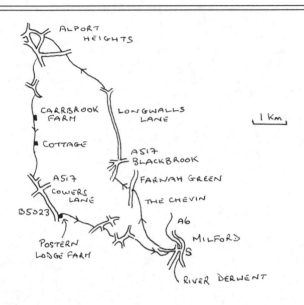

Cross the bridge and go up narrow Chevin Alley. Cross Chevin Road and go up Sunny Hill, climbing steeply out of **Milford**. The metalled road becomes an unmade track as you pass a trig. point in a field on the right. Continue along the track, going through a golf course and along a ridge called The Chevin. At the T-junction at the track's end, do not turn right down a footpath into Chevinside: instead, turn left along a short lane to Farnah Green Road. Turn right here to reach the Blue Bell Inn. The walk turns left along Farnah Green Road for 100 yards to reach a signed footpath on the right. Follow this to Fearn House. There, follow footpath signs across a field. Use steps to cross a wall and walk along the top edge of woodland, through fields, to reach a farm lane. Turn right to Blackbrook and the A517. Turn right along the pavement for 100 yards, then cross, with care, and turn left along Longwalls Lane. This metalled road soon becomes an unmade track as it climbs steeply out of Blackbrook. The lane reaches another at a sharp bend: turn left along the lane for 150 yards to reach another bend and a signed footpath on the right. Cross a field diagonally to a wall beside a line of electricity poles. Go through a narrow wall gap and bear left, uphill. Pass from field to field, using narrow stiles in the walls, to reach a lane. Cross and continue across fields to reach Peat Lane at its junction with Back Lane. Walk along Back Lane to reach a road junction and turn left along Alport Lane, going around Alport Heights to reach a car park above **Alport Stone**. Continue along Chequer Lane, passing the other end of Peat Lane. Opposite the next road on the left, turn right along a farm track. The track becomes a footpath: follow it, still walking with the field edges on your right, to reach Top Lane opposite Lawn Farm. Turn left to the T-junction with Palace Lane. Turn right for 100 yards, then, at a bend in the road, turn right through a gate and follow the path beyond across fields to Carrbrook Farm. Pass to the west of the farm buildings and follow yellow signs across fields, passing a solitary cottage. The path veers right to reach the B5023. Turn left along the road to reach traffic lights at the A517. Cross, with care, and continue along the B5023 for 950 yards to reach Postern Lodge Farm. Go through the farm entrance, cross a stile on the left and follow a fence around the farm, keeping the farm buildings on your right. Follow a farm track to a stile and go diagonally across the field beyond, heading towards woodland. Cross more fields to reach an unmade track leading to a lane (Hob Hill) at Hazelwood. Turn left, uphill, for 200 yards to reach a signed path in a holly hedge. Follow this path through fields and then between houses to reach Hazelwood Hill. Turn right, downhill, to the junction with Spring Hollow. Turn left along Spring Hollow to reach Hazelwood Hall Farm, passing **Hazelwood Spring**. Turn right along the track beside the farm, passing cottages to reach fields. The track narrows to a path and continues beside a stone wall, crossing a golf course to reach a lane leading to Sunny Hill. Turn right and descend Sunny Hill to return to the start.

POINTS OF INTEREST:

Milford – Milford's first cotton mill was built by Richard Arkwright and Jedediah Strutt in 1780. A year later the partnership ended, each partner starting his own empire.
Alport Stone – The stone is tall gritstone pillar left over from the quarrying activities. It is very popular with rock climbers.
Hazelwood Spring – The plaque was erected in 1897 to commemorate Queen Victoria's Diamond Jubilee. Until 1952 the spring was the main local water supply.

REFRESHMENTS:
The Strutt Arms, Milford.
The Blue Bell Inn, Farnah Green.
The Railway Inn, Cowers Green.

Walk 35   **HALL DALE**   3m (5 km)

Maps: OS Sheets Landranger 119, Outdoor Leisure 24.

A short but excellent walk through fine woodland.

Start: At 279633, at the entrance to Hallmoor Wood, opposite
Nether Hall Farm, reached from B5057 north-west of Matlock.

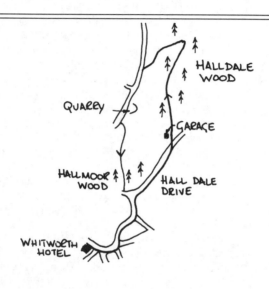

A signpost points the direction up Hall Dale Drive to the north-east. Follow the drive
for about 800 yards to garages on the left. Here, bear left on to a track also signed as
a Public Footpath. Follow the track through Halldale Wood, leaving it leftwards after
about 800 yards to follow a well-trodden path that rises up a hollow. The new path rises
and curves leftwards around a shallow hill. Go over a stile by a gate and cross the field
heading towards a barn. Go round it to reach a stile to the right and go over it to a road.
Turn left and go down the road, past the entrance to Burley Fields Farm and a small
quarry. Just past the quarry, where the road bends right, go left over a stile. Go down
across fields, keeping the wall on your right, crossing three more stiles to reach
Hallmoor Wood. Follow the wide path through the wood, keeping straight on at all path
junctions. The path descends and swings left to emerge back at the starting point.

POINTS OF INTEREST:
Near the start of the walk Millclose Mine was the largest and richest lead mine in Derbyshire. It was closed after severe flooding in 1938. The Whitworth Hotel and Institute was once Stancliffe Hall, but changed its name when it was bought by Sir Joseph Whitworth the engineer who invented the Whitworth thread.

REFRESHMENTS:
Numerous available in nearby Matlock.

Walk 36   **STONE EDGE AND HOLYMOORSIDE**   3m (5km)

Maps: OS Sheets Landranger 119; Outdoor Leisure 24.

A very pleasant woodland walk.

Start: At 342672, a lay-by on the B5057 near its junction with the
A632.

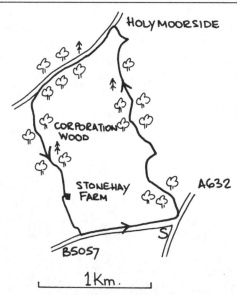

Walk to the main road, turn left and take the path by the bus stop sign painted on a
gatepost. The path goes to the right of the old stone quarry track. Ignore all right and
left turnings, and keep to the main path to the far side of Stone Edge Plantation where
you cross a stile on to a golf course. The path goes downhill over the golf course to a
farm where it turns right to a pond then left down the left-hand side of a wall. Go left
again along the edge of the golf course to enter a wood below the farm, at a sign. (This
is a recent path diversion.) Continue on this path through Gladwin wood to a track, at
the bottom of which go over a stile and down a field. Cross a track, go through a gate
and turn left on a signed footpath. Go left up a drive to the road out of **Holymoorside**.

Turn left and walk up the road for just over ¹/₂ mile. As the road emerges from the
wood look left for a view of **Stone Edge Chimney** on the distant hill. That is the

78

direction of the walk and you will now see a stile on your left just before stone gate posts. Take this path down to a footbridge over the **River Hipper** past old water works and then up through Corporation Wood, crossing a stream. Go past Stonehay Farm and up the farm track to a road. Here you have a close view of the chimney, and a chance of refreshment at the Red Lion, along the road to your left. The lay-by start is a short way further along the road.

POINTS OF INTEREST:
Holymoorside and the River Hipper – The Hipper-powered mills in the village were used for lead smelting and silk and cotton spinning.
Stone Edge Chimney – The oldest free-standing industrial chimney in Britain built around 1770. Site of a cupola for smelting lead ore.

REFRESHMENTS:
The Red Lion, Stone Edge (tel no: 0246 566142).

Walk 37   **PADLEY GORGE** $3^3/_4$m (6km)

Maps: OS Sheets Landranger 110 & 119; Pathfinder SK 28/38 and Outdoor Leisure 24.

A fine, oak-filled rocky gorge.

Start: At 266801, the Longshaw Estate car park.

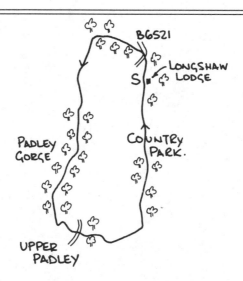

From the car park, follow the path to the estate lodge on the B652. Cross the road and go down the path to Burbage Brook. Go over the brook on a log bridge and go left. At a path junction go ahead. The path goes steeply down through the ancient oak wood of Padley Gorge. Follow the path that runs parallel to the stream ignoring all side turnings. Go through a kissing gate and down a lane past houses in Upper Padley. At a junction turn left and go over the railway bridge to a café. Beyond this go left through a kissing gate and go up to reach a road. Go left along the road and shortly go right over a low stile to reach a path. The path goes up steeply following the stream. Go half-left away from the stream, to join an ancient flagged path. Go over a ladder stile on to a woodland drive. Go left on the track through several woodland stands and past clumps of rhododendrons. Go through a gate to the left of Longshaw Lodge and follow the path beyond around the foot of the **ha-ha** back to the starting point.

POINTS OF INTEREST:
Ha-ha – The low wall here is a 'ha-ha' which held back a formal lawn, preventing access by animals but not spoiling the view.

Walk 38   NORTHERN CHATSWORTH   4¹/₂m (7km)

Maps: OS Sheets Landranger 119; Outdoor Leisure 24.

A magnificent walk in the northern reaches of Chatsworth Park.
Some of the walk is on concessionary paths and these may not
always be open.

Start: At 282722, the car park near the Robin Hood Inn.

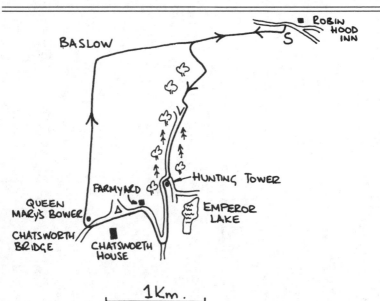

Go back to the main road and turn right for 150 yards. Now cross to a stile and footpath sign. Go over the stile and down steps to a footbridge. Cross over and bear right on to a track. Follow the track along the bottom of Chatsworth Edge to a gate and stile. Go over the stile and the field beyond to another stile into Chatsworth Park (see Walk 57). Follow the wall to the left to the top of the slope and go right above a disused quarry. Go over a stile at the edge of a plantation and go left along the wall to a track. Turn right along the track to a T-junction. Turn right and follow the track (Holmes Lane) down to another junction. Here turn sharp right and downhill to Chatsworth Farmyard. Go past the farmyard and continue, with Chatsworth House on your left, to reach the river at Chatsworth Bridge. Do not cross, but go right before the bridge through a gate to go behind the odd-looking Queen Mary's Bower and along a track towards the Cricket Ground. Continue ahead, ignoring all tracks right and left, to a kissing gate near the northern park entrance. Go right and follow the path signed 'Concessionary Footpath, Robin Hood $1^1/_2$ miles'. This path, a little indistinct at first but becoming clearer, goes over a stile to reach the outward route. Retrace this to the A619 crossed at the start of the walk. Go over and right to the Robin Hood Inn.

REFRESHMENTS:
The Robin Hood Inn, Baslow (tel no: 024 688 3186).

Walk 39   MATLOCK AND BONSALL   5m (8km)

Maps: OS Sheets Landranger 119; Pathfinder SK 25/35 & 26/36.

A fairly hilly walk with some steep hills and marshy areas.

Start: At 297603, the car park at Matlock railway station.

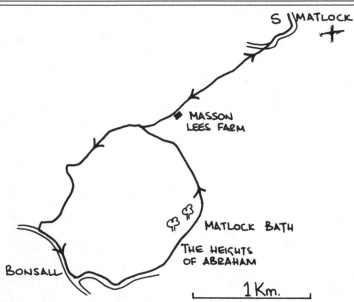

Turn right on to main road and as the road bends to the left turn into Snitterton Road. Go left at the sign for Bonsall via Masson Hill. Continue up steps and go over a stile. Carry straight on over fields, crossing a minor road, and pass to the right of Masson Lees Farm. There is a fine view of Matlock to your right here. At the farm track turn right and in a few yards a footpath sign will be seen to the left. Follow the path up the hill, crossing the track at the top. Shortly after passing a stone barn the path begins to go downhill. Go over a stile and turn left, following the sign for Limestone Way. Follow the path down, taking the right fork. The path goes through trees to reach houses. Just before the first house on the left-hand side go over the stile on your left and down the field to a road. Turn left towards Bonsall and follow the road to the King's Head Inn. Follow the road left towards the school and the church and take the road on the left opposite the church. Follow this road, which becomes a track, passing a turn to the left and go over the brow of the hill. As the track forks near the farm take the right fork, go through a gate and take the footpath on the left signposted 'Matlock'. Follow the path through woods to a stile. The **Heights of Abraham** is on the right. Walkers can enter, but a ticket, purchased in Matlock, is necessary.

Continue straight on, turning right by the cave entrance to join a wider track. Turn right and go down the hill. There are good views of Matlock down to the right at this point. Follow the track past Masson Lees Farm, through a gate and along to the footpath sign on the right. Turn down here, going over fields behind the farm, over the road and down fields to Snitterton Road. The railway station start is now directly ahead.

POINTS OF INTEREST:
Heights of Abraham – Natural rock formation high above Matlock, reached by walking or cable car. Cafeteria, shop. Caverns open to public.

REFRESHMENTS
The King's Head Inn, Bonsall (tel no: 062 982 27043).
The Heights of Abraham Cafeteria (open to non-ticket holders).

Walk 40   MATLOCK AND WENSLEY DALE   6m (9.5km)

Maps: OS Sheets Landranger 119; Outdoor Leisure 24.

A walk on the edge of the National Park. Best at weekends.

Start: At 296603, the car park at Matlock railway station.

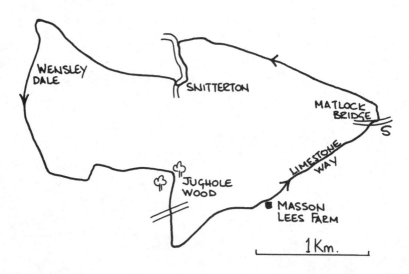

Go to the adjacent Pay and Display car park and take the marked footpath which follows the river for nearly 1 mile passing by various works in an old quarry. Once past this and over a stile bear left over the field to a road. Turn left into Snitterton. Where the road turns sharp left look for the Bull Ring in the road. On the right is a footpath signed for Wensley/Winster. Go through a 'garden' gate and on to another gate following the signpost to Wensley. Head firstly for a trough, then a series of stiles marked in white. After the third stile the path follows a wall to the next stile. Go over this stile and, with the wall now on the right, pass the foot of Northern Dale to a gate into **Wensley Dale**.

    Leave the farm track and head for a stile at the right end of the wall across the dale. Go up the dale to a rise on to a flatter part. (This is where the local school's sports day was held, cowpats having been removed first!) At the foot of the rise climb diagonally back up the left-hand bank. Go straight up the hill to a stile in the left-hand corner of the field. Look back for a good view over Wensley Dale to **Oker Hill** and its tree.

Keep straight ahead, crossing a farm track from Wensley village, to the next stile. Cross the next field diagonally to the right corner and pass through a broken wall to reach a stile, left. From here a path leads to the next stile but keep children close as there is a capped mine shaft next to the path which cavers may have opened. Go over the stile, climb in a straight line uphill, go through a broken wall and up over hummocky ground to a wall at the top. Do not proceed straight ahead but turn left through a stile in the corner of the wall. Keep the wall on your right through the next two fields, then turn left downhill to the wood where you turn right on a clear track. This drops downhill to a gate above Leawood Cottage. Do not go through the gate but continue ahead with the wall on your left through four fields. Here you have a good view of Snitterton Hall (1631). When you reach the foot of Jughole Wood bear right, go through a stile and then right uphill on a path through the wood to pass the **Jughole** cave entrances.

At the top of the wood cross the field to a stile in the right-hand corner and go over it on to the road. Take the path opposite, signposted 'Bonsall', which goes over two stiles to a track. Take the footpath across the track on your left. From here the path is mostly waymarked, either by yellow arrows or the ram's head of the Limestone Way, which is basically a long descent into Matlock. Follow a green lane, cross the next field. Go over a track and cut across the corner of the next field to a stile. Go over a wooden stile, go right at a track, then left on the Limestone Way to Masson Lees Farm. Cross another track and continue the descent over (mostly) marked stiles. On emerging into Snitterton Road, turn right, then left and into the car park where the walk began.

POINTS OF INTEREST:
Wensley Dale – Evidence of lead mining can be seen in the hummocky ground and in the many old mine shafts, some only recently capped. The climb from Wensley Dale to the top of the hill is part of the old Miner's Track from Bonsall to Mill Close mine.
Oker Hill – The sycamore tree on the ridge is called Will Shore's tree after one of two brothers who each planted one and then left the area to seek their fortunes. Will's tree prospered as did he but his brother did not and his tree died. So runs the old legend which was the subject of a sonnet by William Wordsworth.
Jughole – Part of a large system of caves and lead mine workings, reworked for fluorspar in the 1950s.

REFRESHMENTS:
Many places in Matlock.

Walk 41 HOLYMOORSIDE AND OLD BRAMPTON 7m (11.5km)

Maps: OS Sheets Landranger 119; Pathfinder SK 25/35 & 26/36.

A walk in mixed country with views of Chesterfield.

Start: At 338694, in the village of Holymoorside.

Leave the village by Loads Road passing the Lamb Inn and continue up the hill past Chander Hill Lane to a footpath on the right immediately beyond the water works. After two fields follow the lane to the right and at the bridge near the farm keep to the left of the streams to cross at a gate some yards on. Go through the gate and cross to another at the barn. Follow the path to a lane. Turn right through a gate and follow the lane until it turns to enter the farm. In a corner on the left is a stile over the wall. Cross this and then a small paddock. After a second stile turn left at the wall corner. Follow the line of the overgrown hedgerow around the next field to a stile in the far-right corner. Continue along the top of the next field to a signpost and follow the path around the farm to join a minor road. Turn right along the road and turn in towards the next farm to use a stile on the right to enter a field. Skirt the farm buildings and walk directly ahead to a stile followed by a footbridge leading into the wood. Follow the path uphill, ignoring other paths crossing, to leave the wood by a stile under power lines.Follow the edge of the field to a farm road which leads left to join a minor road at Hallcliff Farm. Cross to a stile opposite and after three fields cross the Chesterfield to Baslow road to steps down into a field. Follow the path to enter Wadshelf at a small Methodist church. Turn right down the road marked 'No Through Road' to a gate and stile leading left some 200 yards beyond the houses. Follow the wall changing sides to cross the next field half right and then ahead to a stile near a large tree. Walk through the disused quarry area to a track leading to a minor road near the Royal Oak at Riddings.

Turn left along the road and then right to Wigley, at the crossroads. Before entering the hamlet turn right along a farm track to cross a field with glasshouses and walk around the next field to a stile. Cross this and follow the wall and hedge first on the right and then on its left to a stile to enter a field on the left. Cross this to a metal gate and stile in the corner on the right. Take the path going steeply down through trees to reach a stone footbridge and stile followed by a second footbridge. Cross and turn right to follow the valley down to a footbridge at the top of Linacre Upper Reservoir. Cross and follow the path around the reservoir to the embankment. Take the path through the trees directly ahead and follow it, bearing left, to emerge on the bank of Linacre Middle Reservoir. At the embankment gate bear half right to cross a dip and climb to steps and railings leading right to a gap in a wall. Cross the field to join a bridleway and the road in Old Brampton. Turn left to pass the church and some 200 yards beyond cross the road to reach a bridleway through iron gates. At the T-junction turn left and take a footpath immediately before the farm leading right to cross alongside the farm buildings. At the footpath signpost after two fields continue ahead to the main road. Turn right for 200 yards and cross to a lane on the left which leads between the buildings at Barley House and enters Holymoorside village at a filling station in Pocknedge Lane. Turn right to reach the start.

REFRESHMENTS:
The Royal Oak, Riddings, Old Brampton (tel no: 0246 568092).

Maps: OS Sheets Landranger 110; Pathfinder SK 28/38.
An excellent walk through fields and wooded valleys.
Start: At 231814, the car park in Hathersage.

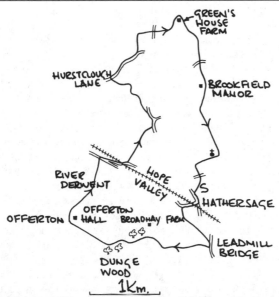

Turn right out of the car park and go first left. Turn right down Dore Lane, go under the railway bridge, and turn left over a stile just before Nether Hall. Go across fields to the main road. Go right over Leadmill Bridge. Go right again through a gap and then over a stile to reach a path along the River Derwent. Just beyond a weir, go left away from the river, over a stile and across to another stile. Go over and uphill to another stile. Go over and turn right along the edge of a field. Go over another stile by a gate and head towards a farm. Go over a stile and right down a track towards Broadhay Farm. Do not reach the farm, going left after crossing a stream go through a gate by a Public Footpath sign. Go across a field, keeping close to the stream. Go over a stile into Dunge Wood and keep ahead to a wall on the right. Turn right through a gate in the wall and continue uphill over a field, past a farm, to a gate. Go through and left along a track. Cross a cattle grid and turn sharp right along a lane. The lane goes uphill, then drops down to Offerton,

90

passing Offerton Hall. Just beyond the hall go right through a gate and then diagonally downhill to a stile. Go over and down to another stile. Go over to reach a signpost. Cross stepping-stones over the River Derwent. (If this is not possible go right along the bank and back to Leadmill Bridge.)

Go up steps, over a stile and left across fields to a road. Turn right. Go left along Hill Foot and over a railway bridge. Now go left up steps between houses and along a narrow path. Where the path ends go over a stile and along a path, crossing several stiles and gates to reach a lane. Go left, bear left at a junction and then turn left through a gate by a Public Bridleway sign for Hurstclough and Bamford. Go along a line of trees to a gate and beyond go left downhill. Go right by a hedge, left, and on down towards trees. Cross a stream and go left to a stile. Go over and go along a track to a gate. The path beyond leads to another gate. Go through and right along a green lane, Hurstclough Lane. After 800 yards the lane bends slightly right. Here cross over a stile in the hedge, and go right along the edge of a field. go over a stile, and on to another stile. Go over and right to a gate. Go through and right across a field to a gate in a wall. Go through, cross a lane and go along a drive. Continue past a house and over a stile to reach a path for Green's House Farm.

Walk behind the farm, through a gate and right over a stile. Go down the field to a gate and on through several more gates to a lane. Cross the lane and go through a gate opposite. Go across a field and along the wall of Brookfield Manor to a stile. Go over and on to a signpost. Go right to join a track to a stile. Cross over this and another. Go left along field edge. Go over a stile and down to a footbridge. Go over a stile and uphill, bearing right at the top to another stile on to a lane. Proceed ahead to Hathersage churchyard.

Turn right in front of the church to continue through the churchyard. Pass through several gates to reach a lane. Go left into the centre of **Hathersage** and cross the main street to a path which leads back to the start.

POINTS OF INTEREST:

Hathersage – The village was a centre for the pins and needles industry in the 19th century, but is more famous for its association with Little John, of Robin Hood fame. His grave, so it is said, is in the churchyard. Charlotte Bronte stayed at Hathersage and used the name of a local family, the Eyres, for the heroine of her best-known book. The church holds the tombs of several members of the Eyre family.

REFRESHMENTS:

Numerous in Hathersage.

Walk 43   AROUND SOMERSALL PARK   7m (11km)

Maps: OS Sheets Landranger 119; Pathfinder SK 26/36 & 27/37.

A walk in varied countryside with easy ascents.

Start: At 355702, the car park in Somersall Park.

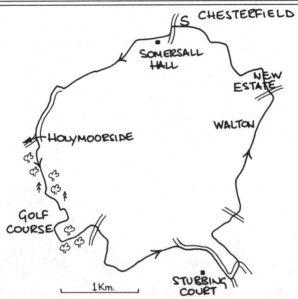

Leave the car park and go left down Somersall Lane to a stile in the hedge on the right. Go over and shortly before the end of the second field cross the ditch to the left using a footbridge. Cross the next field on a well-marked path and continue across fields to a stile in the far corner of the third field, where the hedge ends at a stream. Follow the path along the stream keeping to the same bank until you reach Holymoorside by a bowling green. As the lane from the bowling green joins the main road turn left past the recreation ground and the Bull's Head Inn to leave the village by New Road. Shortly after the school is passed the road levels off and becomes Harewood Road which is followed for some 200 yards to a narrow lane to the left. This leads steeply down to a bridge over the stream. The path passes to the right of a building and through trees to a gate into a sloping field. Climb the slope, crossing a farm road, to a track going uphill between walls at the edge of a wood. At a gate at the top of the track follow the path to the right to Stanedge Golf Course. Follow the edge of the golf course to the left and turn right at a pond. Follow the path to a gate near a farmhouse where a sign indicates a footpath to the left directly across a fairway. Follow this but cross the fairway a few yards further on – in line with the farmhouse – to reach a stile in the wall along the boundary of the golf course marked by a square sign erected by the club. Go over the wall, turn left and follow the path along the line of the wall to join a road. Cross the road and walk left to the top of a farm road leading right down the hill. Follow this to Stone Edge Farm and, in the farmyard, take the gate to the left immediately after the new barn. Follow the edge of the field to a stile and gate leading to a farm road at a broiler house. Turn left down this road passing the broiler houses and a weighbridge and continue as the road becomes a public road through a ford and past the back and front drives of Stubbing Court to reach Stubbing Pond.

Cross the embankment of the pond and at the end turn left (signed 'Wingerworth') to a gate on the left at a bend. Take the path signed 'Harper Hill $^1/_2$ mile'. Keep to the top of the field and, after passing through trees cross a stile in a wire fence on the right.Follow the left hedge to a stile in the corner. *Do not* take the second stile on the left but go into the field on the right and follow the left edge to reach a road after two further stiles. Cross the road and use a step stile in the opposite wall to enter a small field. After crossing the stile ahead follow the wall to the left to a gate and walk along the top of the field to a stile in a hedge. Cross the next field going slightly downhill to an opening in a wall into the trees. The path leads to a stile in a wire fence. Cross this and take the path ahead and to the left of a small stream to a broad grassy track through the trees. This track, after crossing a forestry road, leads to a footbridge at the edge of Walton Golf Course. Follow the path between fences across the golf course and, after crossing a small stream, bear right, then left to follow a line of trees and a hedge uphill to a path between houses at the top of the course. Turn left at the drive along the top to Matlock Road opposite the Blue Stoops. The area between here and Somersall Park has been extensively developed and most of the way is through the estate. Take the road to the right of Blue Stoops, Foljambe Avenue, and follow it until Greenway. Go left on Greenway until, 10 yards after passing Lindrick Gardens, there is a footpath to the right. Follow this to Deben Close and Thorndow Way to reach shops. Take the road to the right of the shops, Walton Close, to reach a footpath which is followed to the right to Somersall Park. Enter the park and cross left to the far corner to reach the start.

REFRESHMENTS:
The Bull's Head Inn , Holymoorside (tel no: 0246 568022).
The Blue Stoops, Brookside (tel no: 0246 73689).

Walk 44   **ASHOVER AND LITTLEMOOR**   7m (11km)

Maps: OS Sheets Landranger 119; Pathfinder SK 26/36.

A varied, mostly flat walk.

Start: At 351632, the Parish Hall, Ashover.

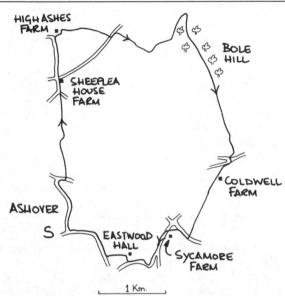

Turn left out of the car park and right in to Moor Road. Opposite the Post Office turn right and follow the road uphill until a paved path with a handrail joins from the left. Take the path opposite up through trees to a minor road and turn right to a stile on the left after some 20 yards. Go over and at a gate go over another stile to the left and continue along the wall on the other side. At the next stile cross the fields, to a stile half left and, in the next field, cross half right to a stile in the far-right corner. Go over to a road junction. Follow the road left, signposted 'Wingerworth', and at a crossroads go directly ahead to a farm on the rise. Turn into the farm and cross the yard to a gate in the far corner which leads to a paddock and a stile which uses a dead branch to increase its height. Follow the track beyond through fields to a gate. Press Reservoir can be seen half-right.

At the gate continue ahead to a gate to Birkin Farm and the road. Turn left at the road and, after 100 yards, right down a farm road with views over Chesterfield to the left. Pass the pub to reach a stile on the left, near a concrete telephone post and almost hidden by small trees. Go over and cross a field to a stile at the foot of a large oak tree. From there cross the following field slightly right to a stile near a gate in a dip. Follow the path left along the hillside rising to a wall along the edge of the wood. Follow the wall to a steep road. Turn right uphill and follow the road until it bends sharp right. Cross a stile ahead to enter woods. Follow the broad path along the top of the woods to a stile, almost hidden by holly bushes, leading to fields. Follow a path through fields, with Clay Cross slightly left ahead, to enter a wood in the field corner. Take the left-hand path to cross a gap in a wire fence to a gate near the Ashover road. Turn left to join the Ashover road and then right for a short distance to a narrow lane, left, leading to Coldwell Farm. At the farm turn right into the yard and right again to pass behind the buildings to a track through fields beside woods to the right. Where the track ends continue ahead to the road at Woodland Lane. Turn right for 100 yards and at a gate on the left cross a field to the road at Sycamore Farm. Turn left and follow the main road through Littlemoor to a narrow road branching right as the road curves left near two tall trees. Follow this road steeply down to the remains of **Eastwood Hall** and turn right between the hall and farm buildings to enter a field. Turn left and follow the path to a road. Turn right for $1/4$ mile to return to the start of the walk.

POINTS OF INTEREST:
Eastwood Hall – A ruined manor house still partly used as a dwelling house.

REFRESHMENTS:
Several in Ashover.

Walk 45　LINACRE WOODS AND MILLTHORPE　$8^{1}/_{4}$m (13km)

Maps: OS Sheets Landranger 119; Pathfinder SK 27/37.

A varied walk in rolling countryside.

Start: At 327727, the Linacre Woods car park.

Leave the car park and turn right downhill to a path, left, to an opening in a wall. Cross the field to a stile. Go over to a broad track through trees to a field at a wooden fence. Cross the field to join the road near the Peacock Inn. Turn right along the road to a track, left, immediately past an old stone house, three storeys high with a tower. Follow the track to a gate and cross the field slightly right to a stile. Cross the brook and skirt trees to a gap in the hedge leading to a footbridge. The path now follows the line of the hedge uphill to a road, crossing two stiles on the way. Turn left along the road for 30 yards to some narrow steps to the right leading between houses to a stile. At the stile turn half-left to a gate at a large tree, then follow the wall first on its left and then on its right to drop down to a road on the edge of Barlow. Turn right along the road passing the Hare and Hounds Inn and then go left at a sign down a walled path into the village. Turn left through the village and take the road to the right after the Post Office. Follow this road until at a sharp S-bend at a small bridge, a road branches left. Take this road and after 100 yards turn right to follow a bridleway towards Cartledge Hall. The bridleway itself is extremely muddy but a path using the fields to the right of the bridleway provides a better route. Follow this until it is possible to rejoin the bridleway at the second gate beyond a wall stile. As the bridleway swings right to Cartledge hall Farm take a path, left, on the bend. The signpost is almost hidden by trees. Cross one field and then turn left down a track to a double gate. Take the stile into the right-hand field and follow down the left side of the field to a stile and road to join the road, left ,downhill to Millthorpe. This is slightly over half-way and the Royal Oak and the Millthorpe Café are only yards away.

At the crossroads take the road opposite (Mill Lane) and after crossing a ford take the footpath over the wall on the right at the sign for Mill Farm. Cross a footbridge and in the next field keep right to a gate into Rose Wood. Take the path left through the trees until a stile in a fence on the left leads into a field. Cross this towards the buildings ahead and go through a gate to the left of the big tree. At the next gate cross to the small stream and go right up a muddy path to a step stile on to a track. Cross the track to a stile leading into an overgrown area which is crossed to the left to a gate leading between farm buildings. This farm road leads to a public road at Allen Wood. Turn left for 30 yards and then right at the road sign 'Barlow 2 miles'. Immediately after crossing a bridge in a hollow take the gate on the right and follow the path rising to the left to cross a field to a stile in the wall at the top. Cross the next field to an opening in the middle of the far side and after a further field reach a minor road at Grange Lane. Turn left and immediately right through a farmyard to follow a bridleway to where a path crosses in a dip. Take the path to the left and after a double stile skirt a concrete storage area and cross diagonally at the rear of the house to an opening in a wall near a liquid gas storage tank. Through the opening the path passes poultry pens to a small stream passing under the path, and a stile. Cross the small field to exit over a stile well hidden by holly bushes in the top corner ahead. At the gate on to the bridleway turn left and then left again at the minor road to follow this through Oxton Rakes to join the main road at the Gate Inn. Turn left for some 200 yards and take the road to the right. Shortly after the houses end, a footpath leads right across a field to a squeeze stile. After a further stile the path bears left through a fence into Linacre Woods. Follow the broad path down to the end of the reservoir embankment and then left to a gate at the next reservoir embankment. Shortly after the gate, wooden steps among the trees lead to the starting point.

REFRESHMENTS:
The Royal Oak, Millthorpe (tel no: 0742 890870).

Maps: OS Sheets Landranger 119; Outdoor Leisure 24.

A short walk around a most interesting town.

Start: Any one of several car parks in Bakewell.

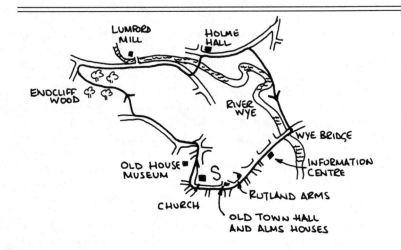

Reach the town **church**. Go west past it to reach Church Lane. Go right. To the left is a lane down to **Old House Museum**. Ahead is a YHA building to the right. Go on to a T-junction and there go left, bearing right into Stonedge Road. At a footpath sign go right across the playing fields and through Endcliff Wood to reach a road at a T-junction. Go right, passing the gas works to reach Lunford Mill (across the river) an old cotton mill once powered by a 25-foot diameter water-wheel.

Go down the road and after a right-hand bend go left, crossing the River Wye over Holme Bridge to reach Holme Lane. Go right, passing **Holme Hall** to the left. Take a signed path on the right that leads to a squeeze between the river and the A619, going through two kissing gates and following the river to a gate on to **Wye Bridge**. Go right along Bridge Street passing the Information Centre, in the 17th-century Market Hall, to reach **The Rutland Arms**. Go left around it to reach the Old Town Hall, built in 1602 and the town almshouses built a century later. Continue to a junction and go right along Church Lane back to the church.

POINTS OF INTEREST:

Parish Church – Mainly Norman, through the south porch has some Saxon work and there are two Saxon cross shafts in the churchyard. The Vernon Chapel was built in the mid-14th century and holds the tomb of Sir John Manners and Dorothy Vernon, whose elopement is a fine romantic legend.

Old House Museum – A museum of the town set in a wattle and daub house of the 16th century.

Holme Hall – A Tudor building with a superb terraced and walled garden.

Wye Bridge – One of the oldest bridges in England, dating from around 1300.

Rutland Arms Hotel – It was here that in 1859 a cook got a recipe wrong and by mistake made the famous 'Bakewell Tart' – or so the story goes! Jane Austen stayed in the hotel in 1811, and parts of the area are included in *Pride and Prejudice*.

REFRESHMENTS:

Numerous in the town.

Walk 47 **MIDDLE MOOR** $3^1/_4$m (5km)

Maps: OS Sheets Landranger 110; Outdoor Leisure 1.

A pleasant walk near the River Kinder and over a little-visited moor.

Start: At 035869, the car park at Hayfield bus station.

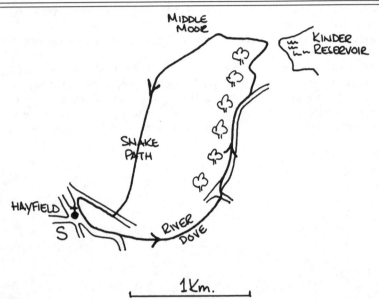

From the car park, take the underpass to the main street and turn right along it. Go left at the top into Valley Road and follow it, even after it becomes a track. From it reach a footpath on the river bank and keep on this to a road. Go left and over a bridge. Go right along a road to the next bridge. Use this to recross the river, leaving the road left to follow the river bank again. This new path leads to another footbridge. Cross the bridge and go over the stile beside the water works buildings and Mountain Rescue Post. Beyond the stile follow a path upwards for about 350 yards to reach another path which goes more steeply upward to reach the top of White Brow. On White Brow the path meets another at a Public Bridleway sign. Go left along the new path to a fork. Take the left fork, signed 'Hayfield', and follow it to a gate. Beyond the gate is the Snake Path which crosses the southern flank of Middle Moor in straightforward fashion, going through several gates to reach a lane in **Hayfield**. Go right along the lane and turn down to the church, beyond which is the bus station and the starting point.

POINTS OF INTEREST:

Hayfield – A pleasant town important as a centre for the textile industry in the 19th century. The Packhorse Inn dates from the 16th century, and recalls the packhorse teams of the 'jaggers' who left the village to cross the northern moors. More recently it was from Hayfield that the mass trespassers on to the grouse moors of Kinder departed in 1932.

REFRESHMENTS:

The Packhorse Inn, Hayfield (tel no: 0663 43671).
There is also a café in Hayfield.

Maps: OS Sheets Landranger 119; Outdoor Leisure 24.

A high moor served with ancient remains.

Start: At 236622, the car park in Birchover.

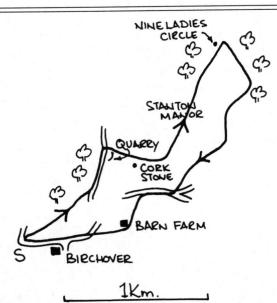

Go through a gap in the wall opposite the Druid Inn and follow the narrow path beyond that heads north-east and upwards to reach a road at a car park. Go left for about 400 yards to reach the entrance to Stanton Park Quarry. Go right over a stile just after a pile of large rocks and across Stanton Moor. Soon you will pass the Cork Stone, a large standing stone near a disused quarry. At a crossroads of paths go left across the open moor. All over the moor at this point there are Bronze Age remains. Follow the path into Stanton Moor Plantation to reach **Nine Ladies Circle**.

Follow the path from the circle for a short distance to reach another path on the right and follow it to a stile. Go over and follow a fence along the edge of the moor. Pass the **Reform Tower** to reach a large standing stone, the Cat Stone. Here the path goes sharp right and then left, passing more stones and dropping down to a lane.

Go right for 200 yards to a Public Footpath sign and stile to the left. Go over the stile and down to a farm. Go left of the farm buildings, through the farmyard and right at a Public Footpath sign. Go right again at the next signpost and over a stile. Bear left to meet a track and follow it to rejoin the lane. Go left back to the Druid Inn.

POINTS OF INTEREST:

Nine Ladies Circle – Stanton Moor must have been an important Bronze Age Centre as over 70 sites have been located there. The major sites are the Doll Tor circle, just off the route to the west, and the Nine Ladies Circle whose 3-foot stones form a circle 35 feet in diameter. To the west is a solitary standing stone known as the King Stone.

Reform Tower – The tower was erected to commemorate the Reform Bill of Earl Grey, a man now more famous for his tea.

REFRESHMENTS:

The Druid Inn, Birchover (tel no: 062 988 302).

Walk 49   **Higger Tor and Carl Wark**   3¹/₂m (5.5km)
Maps: OS Sheets Landranger 110; Pathfinder SK 28/38.
An interesting, easy walk almost wholly in South Yorkshire!
Start: At 263806; the Fox House Inn on the A625, Sheffield to
Hathersage road.

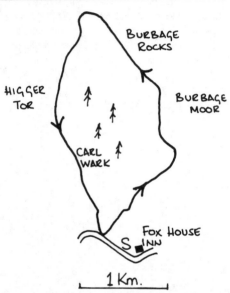

Go towards Hathersage for 500 yards to a footpath sign. Cross over the stile and follow
a grassy track. Pass close to the rectangular block of a partially completed stone trough
and, shortly afterward, an incomplete millstone. Pass to the right of a large rock to the
top of the Burbage Edge and, skirting the old quarry, follow the path along the rocks
until they become scattered. The path here bears left and follows the line of an old wall
to cross a small stream before climbing gradually to the top of Burbage North Rocks.
Following this path you come to a gate on to a minor road. Turn left and continue over
two streams to a stile on the left over a wire fence. (This is often the site for a mobile
refreshment van during the summer months.) Cross the stile and follow the path
through the heather keeping to the top of the slope. After about 400 yards the path

descends a little and then continues level until a short ascent gains the top of **Higger Tor**.

Walk along the left edge to the far end. Before descending use the vantage point to view Carl Wark and its wall. Take the path to **Carl Wark** and climb the slope to the left of the wall. Cross the plateau and descend the obvious path to the stream. (The crossing can be wet and muddy and an alternative is shown on the map.) From the stream crossing, the path leads to a track and a gate back to the starting point.

POINTS OF INTEREST:

Higger Tor – Described in archaeological books as a gritstone bastion. It may be associated with Carl Wark.

Carl Wark – An Iron Age hill fort in the form of a plateau guarded by natural rock defences on three sides with the other, more vulnerable, side protected by a wall of large blocks which appear to have been used in their natural state.

REFRESHMENTS:

The Fox House Inn (tel no: 0433 30374).

Walk 50 **EDALE AND MAM TOR** 3¹/₂m (5.5km)

Maps: OS Sheets Landranger 110; Outdoor Leisure 1.

Although short the walk starts with nearly 1,000ft (300 metres)
of climbing. Spectacular views.

Start: At 125853, the car park in Edale.

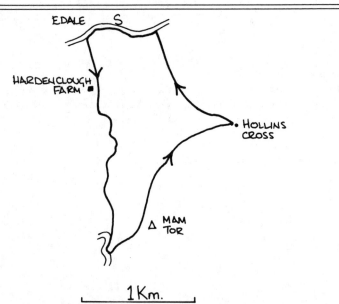

Turn right out of the car park along the road, going past the right turn to Edale village
to a farm road on the left signed 'Hardenclough Farm'. Keep to this road past the farm
as it bends left then right to Greenlands. Take the footpath on the left signed 'Mam Tor'.
Keep to the main path through a gate and continue up for about ³/₄ mile to a road at Mam
Nick. Turn left on the road, then left up newly-made steps to the summit of **Mam Tor**.
Keep children under close control as the cliff face drops down to your right.

Follow the ridge path to **Hollins Cross** where there is a viewfinder table and a
junction of old packhorse ways. Take the left-hand of two paths down to your left then
the right-hand fork signed 'Edale'. This joins a farm track at **Hollins**. Follow this track
down over the River Noe to the road, where you turn left for the car park and station.

POINTS OF INTEREST:

Mam Tor – Topped by an Iron Age hill fort dating from c. 5th century BC. Known as the Shivering Mountain because of serious landslips over the years.

Hollins Cross – Several old packhorse routes meet here including the old road from Castleton to Edale walked each day (weather permitting) by Castleton mill-girls. The Edale Mill buildings can be seen from the ridge.

Hollins – A traditional Derbyshire farmhouse, living quarters one end, animals the other under one long ridge.

REFRESHMENTS

The Nag's Head Inn, Edale (tel no: 0433 70212).

Walk 51   **DARLEY DALE AND SYDNOPE DALE**   4m (6.5km)

Maps: OS Sheets Landranger 119; Outdoor Leisure 24.

A very pleasant, varied walk.

Start: At 270624, the Darley Bridge picnic site.

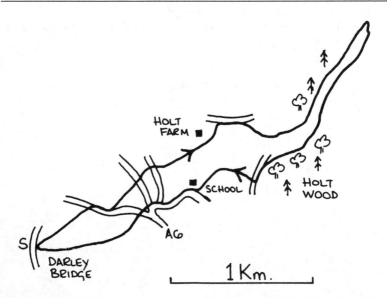

Turn right out of the car park, cross the road and proceed to Flatts Farm just before **Darley Bridge** over the River Derwent. Take the left-hand of two stiles. (Your return walk emerges at the right-hand stile. From here you can see the full extent of the walk up the right-hand of two wooded valleys, hence the modern name of the village at their foot – **Two Dales**.)

Cross the field in the direction of steps up a bank at the far side. Turn right on the road at the top of the steps then left along the right-hand side of the grounds of the new DFS Store. Cross Warney Brook and follow the wall to the A6 which you cross to a footpath directly opposite. Follow this path by the side of Forest Nurseries, across a lane, on over Warney Brook and over a stile. Go left to a stile across the field. Go over the next field and ahead down a track to a road. Turn right along the road past the former mill (built in 1826 for flax spinning) and into the wood. Here there are various paths, rocks and dams to explore, but the walk keeps to the main path ahead, passing three dams to a waterfall. Here climb up steeply to your right, keeping right where the path forks, then bear left to the edge of the wood and a gate. Turn right again, back through the wood at a higher level, with good views over Darley Dale to Stanton Moor. Leave the wood and continue past Holt Top Cottage. Take the signed footpath on the right down hill to a stile. Cross the field to two gates where you turn left along the wall, down a lane past houses to a road. Turn right on the road which bends left and leads down to the A6. Cross the road and continue opposite to the Red House Hotel. Take a footpath on the left-hand side of the wine bar, which crosses the **railway**.

After crossing Warney Brook go over a stile in the fence on your right and across to a stile in the far corner of the field, past a meander of the River Derwent. The path now bears right over stiles to Flatts Farm and the road, where you turn right past the Square and Compass for the car park.

POINTS OF INTEREST:

Darley Bridge – An old packhorse bridge, still with two original pointed arches, but widened on its upperside for modern traffic.

Two Dales – Until late 19th century the village was called Toadhole.

Railway – This section of the line was relaid in 1989 and is used by steam trains of the Peak Rail Society.

REFRESHMENTS:

The Red House Hotel (tel no: 0629 734854). Wine Bar and coffee shop. There is a carriage museum here also.

The Square and Compass (tel no: 0629 733255). Morning coffee.

Walk 52   DEEP DALE FROM CHELMORTON   4m (6.5km)

Maps: OS Sheets Landranger 119; Outdoor Leisure 24.

A walk of contrasts.

Start: At 114702, near Church Inn, Chelmorton.

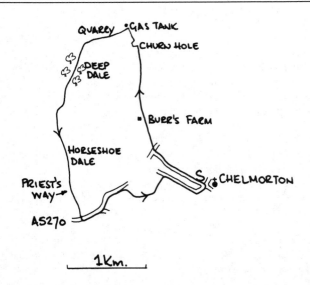

Go down the lane opposite which is marked with a footpath sign. Cross the road at the bottom and take the right-hand lane. Follow this to a stile. Go over into a field and follow a path that goes to the right of Burrs Farm. Beyond the farm the path goes down a section of slippery path into Marl Dale. Please be careful. At a gas storage tank go left around the quarry. Go up a steep bank and left of a slurry lagoon. There is a warning notice here. Please read it and be careful.

The path now goes through the beautiful, narrow Deep Dale. Where the path forks go left on a wide path along the bottom of Horseshoe Dale. The path here is known as Priest's Way, probably because the land was owned by a monastery before the Dissolution. Go uphill, through a yard to reach a gate. Go through on to a road. Turn left and follow the road for about 400 yards going past a road that leads to the right for Chelmorton. At a black iron shed go right along a narrow track. Follow this through the ancient Chelmorton field system, going diagonally left when it ends to reach another track. Follow this to a road. Go right and back to Chelmorton.

REFRESHMENTS:
Several available in Chelmorton.

Walk 53   CRESSBROOK DALE   4$\frac{1}{2}$m (7km)

Maps: OS Sheets Landranger 119; Outdoor Leisure 24.

An interesting walk along a quiet dale. The path out of the dale is steep and indistinct.

Start: At 182756, the Three Stags Head, Wardlow Mires.

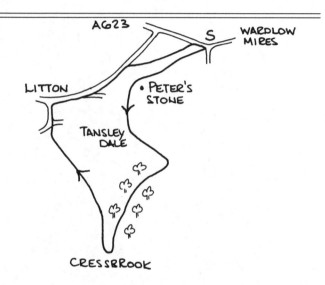

From the pub go west to the T-junction. Go through a gate opposite between a cottage and an outbuilding. The path passes underneath Peter's Stone, a knob of limestone beyond which, after about 800 yards, you take the well-trodden path which forks left and up. At the top of the valley there is another fork. Go right and back down to the stream and a footbridge. Cross and climb up, keeping to the left of a wall and wood. The footpath becomes wider and reaches woodland. Go into the wood for a few yards to reach a footpath sign 'Litton'. Take this and, ignoring all footpaths that level out, climb up steeply through trees. At the top of the climb go right along a narrow footpath for 400 yards to a stile. Go right and cross fields and stiles to reach a track. Cross to a stile opposite and continue over more fields and stiles to a road. Follow this to a junction in Litton. Turn right (the Red Lion is to the left) for $\frac{1}{2}$ mile to a stile on the right. Go

112

over and take the path that leads back to the A623. When this is reached turn right to the start.

REFRESHMENTS:
The Three Stags Head, Wardlow Mires (tel no: 0298 721251).
The Red Lion, Litton (tel no: 0298 871458).

Walk 54   **FLASH** $4^{1}/_{2}$m (7km)

Maps: OS Sheets Landranger 119; Outdoor Leisure 24.

A relatively easy walk in a fine position.

Start: At 025672, the village of Flash.

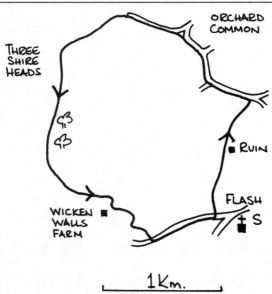

Go past the New Inn and the former Wesleyan chapel on the right. Take the first track on the right, and follow it to a fork. Take the right fork and follow the track to a ruined building. Go past the ruin and bear left across two fields to a stile in the corner of the second field. Go over and head for a boundary stone ahead. Beyond this is a stile in the fence on the right. Go over to reach a track. Follow it to a lane. Turn left along the lane for $^{1}/_{4}$ mile to a T-junction. Turn right and follow the road until it descends to the right. Leave it here to follow a wall on the left to reach the road again. This manoeuvre cuts a corner. Then left along the road. The metalled surface soon ends and you follow a rough track to Pannier's Bridge at **Three Shire Heads**.

    Do not cross the bridge but turn left downstream, following the left bank of the River Dane. After a few hundred yards the track forks. Take the upper track and follow it, for about a mile, passing several cottages. You will reach Wicken Walls Farm below and right of the track, turn sharp right along the farm track and head for a gate and stile on the left of the buildings. Go over the stile and along a disused, walled track to a footbridge. Cross and turn right. The path becomes a track at another farm and is followed to a road. Turn left and walk steeply uphill back to **Flash**.

POINTS OF INTEREST:

Flash – Once described as a 'harsh village of weatherworn cottages'. Given its height (at 1,518 feet it claims to be the highest village in England) and the winter climate, this is hardly surprising. Once the village had a reputation for forged or 'Flash' money.

Three Shire Heads – This beautiful spot is the meeting of Staffordshire, Derbyshire, and Cheshire. It is the meeting place of two streams, each crossed by a packhorse bridge. Panniers Bridge is named for the carrying panniers of the horses.

REFRESHMENTS:

The New Inn, Flash (tel no: 0298 22941). Children admitted, beer garden, snacks available.

Walk 55   **SOLOMON'S TEMPLE**   4$\frac{1}{2}$m (7km)

Maps: OS Sheets Landranger 119; Outdoor Leisure 24.

An easy walk to a fine viewpoint.

Start: At 050725, the car park at Buxton Country Park and Poole's Cavern.

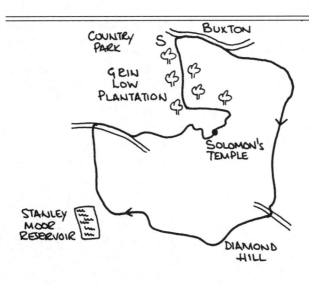

Go back along the road towards the town and right through a gap between houses. Go through several fields to reach a metalled drive. Go right along it to some houses. Cross a cattle grid and turn right over a stile. Turn left and follow the wall uphill staying to the right of Fern House and the woodland beside it. Go over the crest of the hill to reach a road. Go left and down into a hollow. Now cross the road and go right through a gate on to a farm track. Follow this through the farmyard and on to moorland fields. Follow the track straightforwardly across the moor for about 1 mile, passing close to the tip of Stanley Moor Reservoir. The track reaches a road. Go right and follow the road for 400 yards. Go left at a signpost, following a track uphill. You will pass a group of farm buildings, beyond which the direction is given by another signpost. **Grin Low Tower** now gives the line. From the tower go down a wide track to Grin Plantation. Enter the

116

wood over a stile and follow a wide path down, ignoring all side paths. Turn right at steps and follow them to the car park.

POINTS OF INTEREST:
Grin Low Tower – The tower, also known as Solomon's Temple, is a superb viewpoint. It was built in 1895 for a local Buxton man, Solomon Mycock.

REFRESHMENTS:
Many in Buxton.

Walk 56   LONGNOR AND EARL STERNDALE   4¹⁄₂m (7km)

Maps: OS Sheets Landranger 119; Outdoor Leisure 24.

An interesting route through beautiful countryside.

Start: At 088649, in the village of Longnor.

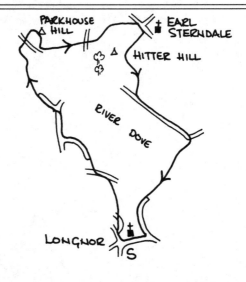

From the village square, go up Buxton Road to Church Street. Now go along the narrow lane that joins Church Street near the main road. Where it goes left in front of bungalows take the footpath, right, to reach a stile on the left. Go over, along the bungalows and then ahead, over a field to a stile. Go over and left downhill to a track. Go left along it for 200 yards to a farm building. There leave the track and go right of the building to reach a stile in the hedge on the right. Go over, pass a house and follow a track for 400 yards to a road. Go right and take the first track on the left. Go over two stiles and after the second bear right downhill to a footbridge. Cross and continue to a stile on to a track. Parkhouse Hill is directly in front of you now should you wish to climb it for the fine views it offers.

Go along the track, leaving it to the left to reach a gate and stile. Go ahead to another stile. Cross the road to a stile, go over and bear left up Hitter Hill. Go over a stile near the top and bear right through fields to Earl Sterndale (see Walk 67). Go right into the village to reach the Quiet Woman pub. Go around it to the right, and follow the footpath, signed 'Crowdecote', through fields to reach a second signpost and then a stile with a handrail. Go over and follow the wall, left, for 50 yards, then go right and downhill to a stile. Go over on to a track by a cottage. Go left along the track for $^1/_2$ mile to where it bends sharp left. Turn right on a path signed 'Longnor', and follow it to a footbridge over the River Dove. Go ahead uphill to a barn. There, turn left and follow the track up into Longnor and the start.

REFRESHMENTS:
The Cheshire Cheese, Longnor (tel no: 0298 83218).
The Crewe & Harpur Arms, Longnor (tel no: 0332 700641).
There is also a café at Longnor.
The Quiet Woman, Earl Sterndale (tel no: 029 883 211).

Walk 57   CHATSWORTH PARK AND BEELEY MOOR   5m (8km)

Maps: OS Sheets Landranger 119; Outdoor Leisure 24.

An easy walk with an interesting variety of scenery.

Start: At 258686, the car park, Calton Lees, Chatsworth Park.

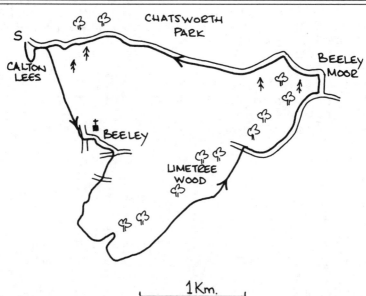

Leave the car park towards the Garden Centre (well worth a visit) and turn left on to a path through trees to the road and bridge. Cross the bridge and go through the swing gate on the right to follow a clear path across a large field to a gate and road. Walk down the lane opposite to a T-junction. Turn right and then left at a fork in the road. Go first right to cross a stream and a stile. Ascend the hill slightly left for 30 yards and then go right to a gap in the hedge by an unused stile. Keeping straight ahead, pass through a gate to cross a road and stile. Follow the Public Footpath sign direction. Turn immediately left over two stiles to pass Fold Farm on the right and go over two further stiles. Two-thirds of the way across the next field, turn left over a stile then right over another. Follow the right boundary hedge to a further stile and walled track. Ascend the track and go through the gate at the top. Turn left along a clear path through a wood. At a path junction in 100 yards turn right and after 200 yards pass between two high stone buttresses. Keep ahead on the path between the quarry on the left and the waterfall on the right. Pass through a gate to follow the path by a stream to the end of the left boundary wall and a farm track. Turn left on to the track and follow the path line through a succession of gates to the road. Walk up the road right for $^1/_2$ mile to the end of the trees and turn left on to a wide track between walls. Here are fine views of **Beeley Moor**, East and Gibbet Moors with evidence of pre-historic man seen in several tumuli and cairns spread over them. The track descends for $1^1/_2$ miles back to the main road passing, en route, through the hamlet of Beeley Hilltop. Cross the river bridge and ascend the path through the trees to the car park at **Chatsworth Park** where the walk began.

POINTS OF INTEREST

Beeley Moor – Site of the well-known Hob Hursts House, a barrow (tumulus) which is square, with a square ditch and bank.

Chatsworth Park – The magnificent setting for Chatsworth House, 'The Palace of the Peak', internationally famous for the splendour of its design and contents and gardens. There is also a working farm exhibition.

REFRESHMENTS:

The Devonshire Arms, Beeley (tel no: 0629 733259).

Walk 58   **Baslow and Birchen Edge**   5m (8km)

Maps: OS Sheets Landranger 119; Outdoor Leisure 24.
Gritstone edges and part of Chatsworth Park.
Start: At 258722, Baslow car park.

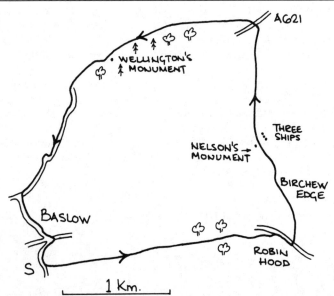

Turn right out of the car park, go over the bridge and right past a thatched cottage (very unusual in the Peak District) along a path into Chatsworth Park (see Walk 57). Here you find a map showing concessionary paths which do not correspond to the White Peak map. Turn left up hill following a signpost to Robin Hood. Cross the road from the Golden Gates and head for a large boulder named Jubilee Rock on the White Peak map. Keep in a straight line and you will reach a gate and stone step stile. Follow the track beyond, climb another step stile and, ignoring a turning to the road, go over another stile. Now fork left and down a path, to a footbridge, not marked on the map. Go over and up steps to the road A619. Cross the road, turn right and then take the left turning past the Robin Hood Inn and the adjoining car park (an alternative start) to the ladder stile on the left. From here various paths go for about 1¹/₂ miles through access land at Birchen Edge. Now either turn right up to the top of the edge on a well-trodden steep path soon after the ladder stile and continue along the top to the trig. point where you follow a path down through the rocks or continue a little further along the low path until you come to a path forking right. Take this along the foot of the cliffs to rejoin the top path below the trig. point. The trig. point is beyond **Nelson's Monument** and the **Three Ships**. The rocks are very popular with rock climbers.

The path continues down over rather boggy ground to a road junction. Turn left over a stile, cross the main road (A621) and continue ahead to a gate. Go through the gate and follow the track to Wellington's Monument, where there are extensive views of the Edges. The fountain at Chatsworth can also be seen. Ignoring two paths to the right, keep to the Edge path which goes gradually down hill, turning first to a walled track and then to a road. Turn left at the T-junction and continue down to the main road at Baslow where tea rooms are open in the tourist season. The car park is opposite.

POINTS OF INTEREST:
Nelson's Monument – Erected in 1810 to celebrate Trafalgar and to commemorate Nelson's death.
Three Ships – Near the monument are three huge rocks resembling three ships and named Victory, Defiant and Royal Sovereign. The rocks are very popular with rock climbers.

REFRESHMENTS:
The Robin Hood Inn , Baslow (tel no: 024 688 3186).

Walk 59   **GREAT SHACKLOW WOOD**   5m (8km)

Maps: OS Sheets Landranger 119; Outdoor Leisure 24.

A delightful walk through woodland and a quiet dale.

Start: At 171706, the White Lodge picnic area, Monsal Dale.

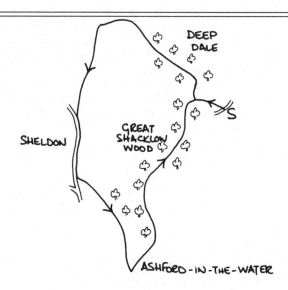

1Km.

Go over a stile on the south side of the picnic area and follow a footpath. Go over another stile and on to a fork in the path. Take the right fork through Deep Dale for a mile to reach a wall. Go through a gate on the right and on for 70 yards to a stile, on the left. Go over and up the valley side to a stile at the top. Go over and follow the wall on the left through several gates. Where the wall turns sharp left go left to a stile, cross and continue to reach a road over a stile by a gate. Go left along the road to Sheldon. Go through the village to reach a point where the road dips. Go left over a stile to reach a path. Where it forks, take the higher path to the right and follow it down through fields and over stiles, bearing slightly right. Head for Ashford, visible ahead and turn left along the footpath on the bank of the Wye. (To reach the refreshments in Ashford go right along the path, over a stile and left to the road. Turn right and take the first bridge over the river into the village.)

Follow the river path, passing an old mill, to reach Great Shacklow Wood. Go over a stile to reach the outward path which is retraced to the start.

REFRESHMENTS:
The Bull's Head, Ashford (tel no: 0629 812931).
The Ashford Hotel, Ashford (tel no: 0629 812725).
There is also a café at Ashford.

Walk 60   ELTON AND BIRCHOVER   5¹/₂m (9km)

Maps: OS Sheets Landranger 119; Outdoor Leisure 24.

A well-marked walk with some steep gradients.

Start: At 222610, in the village of Elton.

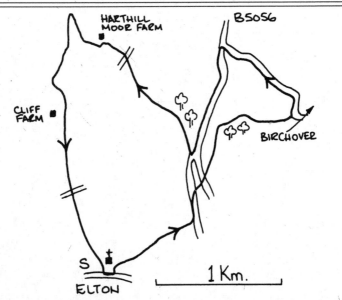

From Elton take the footpath through the churchyard. Cross the lane and continue down the field. When the path forks go right. Follow the field to the bottom of the hill and go over a stile in the bushes to the right. Carry on across fields, keeping telegraph poles to the right, until a road is reached. Turn left, follow the road to a farm. Turn right on the footpath across fields and cross the main road (B5056). Follow the footpath opposite, cross a stream and then follow a footpath up fields and through a wood. Continue around to the right with the top of the hill on the right-hand side. When the path joins a loop in a track, go left and down to Birchover, passing the church. When the road is reached the Druid Inn is on the left, with Druids Rocks behind it.

Turn left and follow the road for just over ¹/₂ mile to meet the main road. Turn left towards Ashbourne. This is the only walking on a main road on this walk. After ¹/₂ mile there is a turn to the right signed 'Access Only'. A footpath goes off to the right towards the rocks. At the stone gateway the track bends right. The footpath carries straight on up the field to pass between the two outcrops of rock. Cross over a stile and go down the field towards Harthill Moor Farm. Cross the road and continue ahead down the farm track. Pass round to the left of the farm and go down the field beside the telegraph poles. At the bottom turn left and follow the poles across fields and beside a wood. Go over a stile off to the right and pass between the copse of trees and Cliff Farm. Shortly after crossing the farm track Elton can be seen ahead. Cross the lane and continue up the fields to join the main road through Elton just to the right of the church, and close to the start.

REFRESHMENTS:

The Druid Inn , Birchover (tel no: 062 988 302). Old-fashioned pub doing bar food and with a restaurant.

The Duke of York, Elton (tel no: 062 988 367). Village pub.

There is also a café in Elton.

BASLOW AND CURBAR   5¹/₂m (9km)

Maps: OS Sheets Landranger 119; Outdoor Leisure 24.

A well-marked walk with varied country from moorland to riverside.

Start: At 258721, the car park in Baslow.

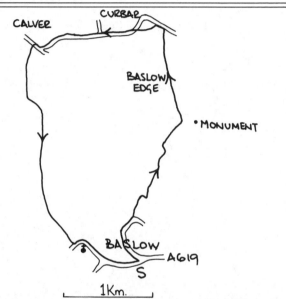

Cross the main road and go up the road opposite. After ¹/₄ mile turn right into Bar Road. Continue uphill as the road becomes a track. At the summit of the hill take the left fork in the path past the flat stone outcrop. The right turn here goes to the Wellington Monument from which the views are superb.

After crossing the top of the ridge go through the gate and turn left on to the minor road. Follow the road for 100 yards and take the footpath on the left. Follow the path downhill and cross a stile to rejoin the road into Curbar. When the road joins the main road turn right. The Bridge Pub is next to the bridge over the river. After crossing the bridge take the footpath on the left which passes under the main road. Follow the path between houses and the river and into open countryside. Continue along the path next to the river for nearly 1 mile until it joins a minor road. Turn left and follow the road past the weir into Baslow. Turn left, go over the bridge and turn right on to the main road. Pass the church and continue to the roundabout. Go past the roundabout to the Sheffield road. The car park is just past the Cavendish Hotel on the right.

REFRESHMENTS:
The Bridge, Curbar (tel no: 0433 30415).

Walk 62   LONGSTONE MOOR   6m (9.5km)

Maps: OS Sheets Landranger 119; Outdoor Leisure 24.

A walk with good views and a few steep ascents.

Start: At 224718, the car park in Great Longstone.

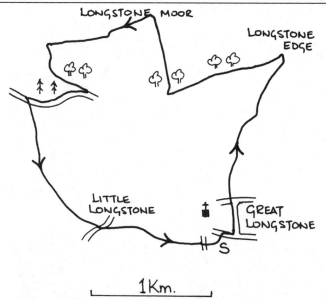

Cross the road and go up Church Lane. Pass the church and after a bungalow on the right there is a footpath. Follow the path diagonally to the right and cross a stile. Continue in the same direction towards a rocky outcrop on the far side of a dip. Go over a double stile and ahead along the valley. Pass through a metal gate on the left opposite a copse of trees. At the end of the valley go across a field to the stile in the top right-hand corner and take the footpath to the right. Walk along the side of the hill to a track and turn right to pass under the power cable. At the junction with the next track turn left uphill and continue to a gate. Turn left and follow the fence for 50 yards to a road. Turn left on to the road and after $^3/_4$ mile, where the road bends left, turn right on to a track and then right on to a footpath signposted 'Longstone Edge'. The path rises sharply to a stile at the top. Follow the path straight ahead on to Longstone Moor.

Go over the remains of a wall and towards a post ahead. Just before reaching the post turn left on to track and go towards two clumps of trees seen ahead. Pass the trees and continue past the fenced-off mineshaft on the right. The path descends here, towards the road past the remains of an old wall. Go to the left of a cattle trough to a path junction. Turn left up towards trees, go over a stile and turn right, with the trees to left. Follow the track left around the edge of the trees and take the right fork down to a stile to a walled area. Turn right into a lane and follow it for $^3/_4$ mile to the footpath signposted 'Little Longstone $^3/_4$ mile'. Follow the path across fields, then cross diagonally to the right-hand wall. Go over a stile and turn left. Follow the ridge of stones to the post and cross the field diagonally right to a stile in the corner. Cross the stile and go over the next stile opposite into a field. Continue towards the large beech trees, go through a gap and over the stile in the wall on the right near the hawthorn. Turn left towards the power line and go through the passageway to the road adjacent to the Packhorse Inn. Turn left and follow the road for 300 yards to the large trees on the right. Take the left-hand of the two paths, signed 'Great Longstone $^1/_2$ mile'. Go over a stile in the fence, over the stile opposite and towards the line of bungalows. Cross the road and take the footpath opposite back to the car park.

REFRESHMENTS:
The Packhorse Inn, Little Longstone (tel no: 0629 87471). Country pub with beer garden. Bar meals available.

Walk 63   **BROWN KNOLL**   6m (9.5km)

Maps: OS Sheets Landranger 110; Outdoor Leisure 1.

A fine walk in the footsteps of history.

Start: At 049869, the car park at the Kinder road quarry.

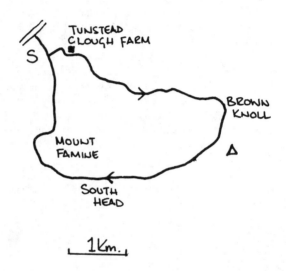

Cross the bridge opposite the car park and go left along the valley road beside the River Sett. Go left and away from the river, through a gate signed 'Tunstead House' and follow drive beyond. Go to the right of the farm buildings, then left up a walled track. Cross over several stiles in walls to reach a kissing gate. Go through and half-right on to a path that rises to a stile. Go over and turn left. Go ahead to reach a gate. Do not go through, but turn right along the wall and fence across Brown Knoll Moor. Ignore stiles in the fence, following the path around the head of the Sett Valley. Keep to the right of some intricate walling, heading for South Head. When you meet a wide track go right along it around the southern side of Mount Famine. The track becomes walled and continues downhill to a corrugated iron shed. Go right now, through a gate and along a path that descends the steep hill leftward to reach a metalled track. Go left along this and back to the starting point.

POINTS OF INTEREST:
A plaque at the car park commemorates the mass trespass of 24 April 1932.

REFRESHMENTS:
Several in nearby Hayfield.

Walk 64   **HARTINGTON AND BERESFORD**   6m (9.5km)

Maps: OS Sheets Landranger 119; Outdoor Leisure 24.

A very attractive limestone dale walk, partly alongside the River Dove.

Start: At 128604, in the square in the centre of Hartington.

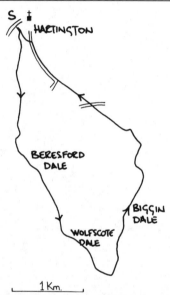

From the square walk past the Charles Cotton Hotel as far as the public toilets on the left where you will see a footpath sign. Go over the stile, bear right and take a well-trodden path over two fields, over a green lane, through two more fields, round to the right of a small peaked hill, Pennilow, and down to the River Dove in Beresford Dale. **Charles Cotton's** fishing house can be seen to your right, as can his prospect tower high above the river, the only surviving remnant of Beresford Hall.

The path crosses a footbridge by pike's pool, the pike being a spire of limestone rock, and follows the Staffordshire bank of the river to Beresford Lane which ends at the river. There the path re-crosses over another footbridge. Continue over the field, not up the track, then at the next footbridge do not cross but keep to the Derbyshire bank through Wolfscote Dale. After about 1$^1/_2$ miles the walk goes to the left up Biggin Dale.

The path crosses the wall in places but do not cross the stile by the small cave, except for investigation! About $1^1/_4$ miles up the dale the path branches. Take the left-hand path, then shortly afterwards another left-hand path signed 'Hartington'. This leads uphill to a track which in turn meets a lane which you follow straight down for about $^3/_4$ mile into Hartington. Near the end you can take a short cut by a footpath on the left, which emerges near to the public toilets.

POINTS OF INTEREST:

Charles Cotton – Friend and later adopted son of Izaak Walton to whose book *The Compleat Angler* he added a second part in the 5th edition. He was the owner of Beresford Hall, now no more, and of the fishing house built 1674. The estate had been in his mother's family (the Beresfords) since Norman times.

REFRESHMENTS:

Various in Hartington.

Walk 65   CASTLETON AND LOSE HILL   6m (9.5km)

Maps: OS Sheet Landranger 110; Outdoor Leisure 1.

A spectacular ridge walk, best in clear weather.

Start: At 149829 the car park Castleton.

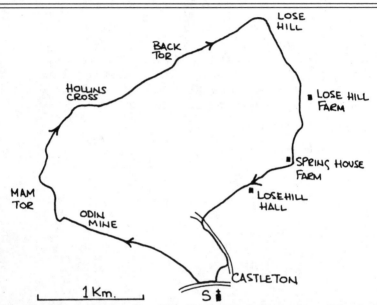

Leave the village in the direction of Mam Tor (see Walk 50). Just beyond the chapel take the footpath on the right which leads up between walls and over a stile. Bear left towards Mam Tor. Go over two stiles, following a stream on the right, then over a double stile on to the Dunscar Farm track. Cross the track and go over the stile almost straight ahead, not the one to your right. The path is now waymarked with yellow painted posts and stiles. Go over a bridge and up to National Trust land, through part of **Odin Mine**, to a road.

    Go right to a notice board explaining the road subsidence. You may make a detour up a path on the left to see the spectacular road damage. Otherwise the walk continues from the point of the road bend down the track behind Mam Farm, left over a stile just before the next house, and gradually up hill to Hollins Cross (see Walk 50). Here there are good views of the ramparts of Mam Tor hill fort, and a viewfinder table.

Continue to the right along the ridge path to Back Tor. Go over a stile to the top of the Tor and on to the summit of Lose Hill. In a dip below the summit is a plaque giving information on Lose Hill. Leave the summit south-east towards Hope, but once over a stile out of the National Trust area bear right to join the lower path from Back Tor which becomes clear as you proceed downhill to the right of a broken wall. Just above Losehill Farm a footpath sign points to Castleton, over a stile and down the wall to a double signpost. Take the left-hand route which continues straight down to a farm track. Follow this past Spring House Farm then turn right past Losehill Hall, a National Park Study Centre. Continue straight ahead over a stile where the track goes to the left and right. Go along the side of the field, over another stile, straight across the next field and bear left on a track. Pass the **Hollowford** Centre and keep left down the road into **Castleton.** The car park is to the right just before you reach the main street.

POINTS OF INTEREST:
Odin Mine – One of the oldest lead mines in Derbyshire. The lead-crushing millstone and circle can still be seen. Across the road in the mine cleft you can see traces of Blue John in the limestone.
Hollowford – This is on the packhorse route (hollow way at the point of a ford) mentioned above.
Castleton – There is much of interest here. A separate day visit is recommended.

REFRESHMENTS:
Numerous opportunities in Castleton.

Walk 66   AROUND HATHERSAGE   6¹/₂m (10.5km)

Maps: OS Sheets Landranger 110 and 119; Pathfinder SK 27/37 and SK 28/38.

A varied walk with excellent views. One short stretch of steep path in Padley Gorge.

Start: The Oddfellows Road car park, Hathersage.

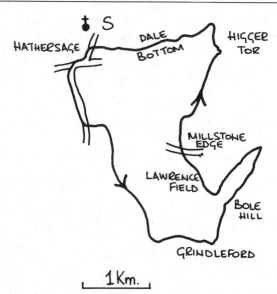

Leave Hathersage by the Grindleford road (B6001) passing the railway station and going under the bridge towards the Derwent. Turn left along the private road to Harper Lees and, just before the house, take the gate on the right into fields. After passing through a further two gates you reach a wooded area, with the path dividing after some 200 yards. Take the left fork up the slope, but before a gate is reached follow the path, to a stile. Go over and take the path across the field passing through gate posts to a clump of trees. Follow the track to the left to cross the railway. The deep cutting in the trees facing the end of the bridge is the **Bole Hill Incline** leading from the old quarries above the railway. Crossing the cattle grid the building on the left is **Padley Hall**, that on the right is for the Peak Park Rangers.

138

Pass the houses, and cross a stream to reach a small opening in the wall immediately beyond a small garage. (At this point a further 100 yards will bring you to the Grindleford Station Café – a worthwhile stopping place.) The walk continues through the gap in the wall. Follow the path through the woods keeping as close to the stream as possible, to arrive at stone steps leading down to a footbridge. Cross and ascend the zig-zag path up the far side until you come to a broad path. Follow this to the right through oak woodland to a gate leading to open ground. There is a junction of paths 200 yards beyond the gate. Turn sharp left back to the trees and follow a path to a small quarry. Enter the quarry and leave by the rocky path up the right side. Follow the wire fence to the left but when the fence turns sharply away continue on the same line across open ground to a wall with the remains of a stone chimney and fireplace standing at a gap. Follow the wall to the right and along the top of Bole Hill and Lawrencefield quarries to a gate to the road.

Turn left and after 50 yards around the bend cross the road to take the first track which leads along the bottom of Millstone Edge. This track finally bends to join a lower track at some old concrete structures. Turn right along the lower track and follow it until it ends. Follow the path leading to open moor. The path follows the side of the hill until Higger Tor (see Walk 49) is almost reached before it drops to a stile on to a minor road. A footpath signpost at a stile on the left, 100 yards right up the road, points the way down to Hathersage. Passing a ruined farmhouse the track rises to join a road at a bend. This road is followed steeply down to the left to Hathersage where, after turning right at the main road, a path immediately opposite the Hathersage Inn leads back to the car park.

POINTS OF INTEREST:

Bole Hill Incline – Was the means by which cut stone for the construction of the Howden and Derwent Dams in the upper Derwent Valley reached the railway. Further up the valley a special railway was built to carry the stone to the construction site, but only traces remain.

Padley Hall – The hall is open Wednesday and Sunday from 2pm (tel no: 0433 30572).

REFRESHMENTS:

The Station Café, Grindleford, is open 8-6 every day except Christmas Day and Boxing Day. It is very much a walkers' and climbers' café providing both snacks and meals. Several available in Hathersage.

Walk 67   EARL STERNDALE AND HOLLINSCLOUGH   7m (11km)
Maps: OS Sheets Landranger 119; Outdoor Leisure 24.
Quieter places, over moorlands and packhorse trails.
Start: At 090670, the Quiet Woman pub, Earl Sterndale.

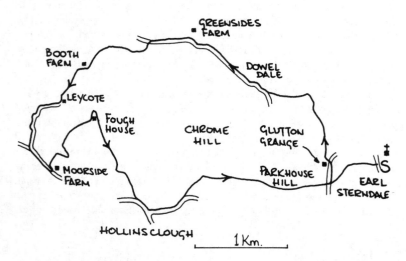

In front of the pub (whose sign is a headless woman!) is a footpath sign. Follow it between the pub and a wooden building, then left between sheds along a footpath signed 'Hollinsclough'. Go over a stile, a field and another stile before crossing a second field to the opposite wall. Turn left along the wall (waymarked) to its corner. Go diagonally right to a stile by a gate. **Parkhouse Hill** with its sharp peak is in the foreground. Cross the stile and field beyond, to another stile with yellow markings. Veer left downhill and go over two more stiles to reach a road. Go right to Glutton Grange. Walk along the Grange drive and turn right on to a stony track. Go through a gate and shortly turn right over a stile. Follow the left boundary wall across two fields and stiles on to a farm track. Turn left up the track, with excellent views including Upper Edge (right) and **Chrome Hill** (left), and, at the top, go right through a gate to cross a stile by a footpath signed 'Dowel Dale'.

140

Cross the field parallel to the right boundary to reach a waymarked stile. Over this the path descends steeply to a road. Go along the road past Greensides Farm (right). Go through a gate before turning left on to Stoop Farm drive. After crossing a cattle grid turn right, as waymarked, to meet a farm track. Turn right along the track to Booth Farm drive. Go up the drive and left to Leycote, visible through the trees. Pass in front of the farmhouse before swinging right uphill. Go down over a well-preserved paved section of a packhorse trail to a packhorse bridge. Washgate is narrow and has low parapets to allow pannier clearance. Over the bridge there are two trails, the walk taking the one straight ahead. First cross the adjacent stream via a footbridge and then climb the hill. The path becomes a green lane between walls and ends at a road. Go up the road for 170 yards and turn along Moorside Farm drive, passing left of the stone barn, to a gate. Pass through and follow the wall to and through another gate. Turn right to descend a grassy path by the left wall. At the bottom go left, passing in front of a disused barn to the wall corner. Turn right and make for the footbridge ahead. Cross the river, ascend the hillside, cross a stile and then another to a gate in a wall. Go through and left in front of Fough House and on to the second packhorse trail. Turn right and, just past the house, take the right fork and follow the trail along the valley side. Cross a stile and descend a waymarked path to a second packhorse bridge. Cross over and go diagonally left across the hillside to a walled path, turning left at its end on to the road in **Hollinsclough**.

After passing the chapel keep left to follow the road past the school before turning first left along a farm track. At a junction, go right, signed 'Glutton Bridge' to cross successively a stile, a footbridge and a cattle grid before reaching another farm track junction. Turn right again and, level with a stile in the right-hand wall, leave the track to go obliquely left across the bottom slope of Parkhouse Hill and over a yellow marked stile. Maintain the same line to cross further stiles and the B5053 road before ascending the hillside to retrace the first section of the walk back to **Earl Sterndale.**

POINTS OF INTEREST:
Parkhouse and Chrome Hills – Limestone reefs formed like the Great Barrier Reef. Chrome, pronounced 'Kroom', looks like a dragon's back from Hollingsclough.
Hollinsclough – The chapel was built in 1801 by John Lomas, a Jaggerman (packhorse train leader). The name derives from the German, *jaeger*, a breed of pack horse.
Earl Sterndale – The prefix Earl indicates it was originally on the estate of William de Ferrers, the Earl of Derby, whereas King Sterndale was on the Crown estate.

REFRESHMENTS:
The Quiet Woman, Earl Sterndale (tel no: 029 883 211).

Walk 68   WIN HILL AND LADYBOWER   7m (11km)

Maps: OS Sheets Landranger 110; Outdoor Leisure 1.

A very fine walk with a succession of beautiful views.

Start: At 201853, the car park near Ladybower Reservoir dam.

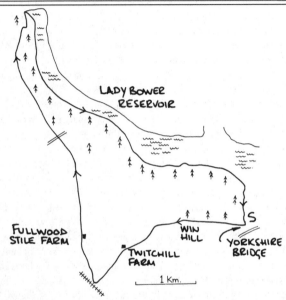

From the park follow the main road down to an inn and just after take a short lane right to Yorkshire Bridge. Go over, and right to a stile. Go over to a track which passes through trees and then goes straight up the side of Win Hill. It is very steep and rugged, but will put you in good shape for the rest of the walk! Towards the top of the tree line the slope eases and a path going over Win Hill is easily picked out. Go south west to a signpost and follow it down to Twitchell Farm. Follow the farm track down to a lane at the side of a rail line and turn right along a footpath to Fullwood Stile Farm. Shortly after the farm a lane leads to a gate which allows passage on to the open hill side. The track climbs steadily along a footpath marked Roman Road and provides constant fine views across to Edale and Kinder Scout.

The track levels at the top of an incline where there are views over a wooded valley and Ladybower to the right. After the cross, and to the right an old gate, there is a grass track. This goes down through woodland to Elmpits Farm. Here the track goes sharp right between almost obscured gateposts and runs along the southern shore of Ladybower passing Underbank Farm and Nether Ashop Farm from where it is possible to go along any of three paths back to Ladybower Dam and Yorkshire Bridge.

Alternatively from Elmpits Farm go over the river Ashop on to the Snake road which can be taken as an alternative to the woodland walk.

POINTS OF INTEREST:

This is one of the finest walks in the Peak District and one where you will stop frequently to take in the many fantastic views. The best vantage point is the summit of Win Hill where the hills around Castleton and over to Kinder in the west are easily picked out.

REFRESHMENTS:

The Yorkshire Bridge Inn (tel no: 0433 51361).

Walk 69   BAKEWELL AND EDENSOR   7m (11km)

Maps: OS Sheets Landranger 119; Outdoor Leisure 24.

A walk that combines riverside meadows, and parkland.

Start: At 220687, the car park near the bridge in Bakewell.

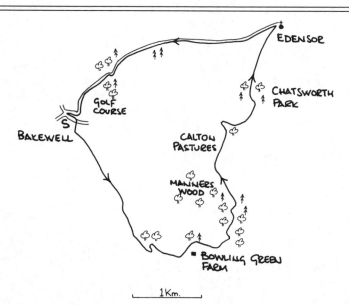

Leave the car park right along a minor road for 50 yards, cross a stile to a fenced path to the river. At the end go left across fields and stiles and then through trees and scrub following the River Wye. At a minor road turn left and shortly after the road turns left over a disused railway tunnel you will see a path, right, signed 'Public Bridle Road'. Follow this to **Bowling Green Farm.**

Turn left along the wall on what soon becomes a rough track but was once the main approach to Haddon Hall before the A6 was built. Follow the track, bearing right at the top of the hill and ignoring the right fork, to a T-junction with a rough road. This road, from Rowsley to Bakewell, was the original turnpike road between the two towns. Cross the old road and go through a gate into Manners Wood, left. Ascend a steep track to join another track for about 100 yards before going right again to reach and follow a stone wall to a gateway. Go through and continue through conifers to a gate in the corner. Just short of this turn sharp right to a stile into Calton Pastures. Ahead is an obvious gap in the trees on the skyline: this is the route. The black and white cottage to the right is **Russian Cottage**.

Descend the hill obliquely left to a bridlepath signpost and follow the arrow across a gully before climbing right to a road running towards Russian Cottage. About 300 yards short of the cottage go left to a gate and into the gap in the trees referred to above. The road through the wood leads into Chatsworth Park with a superb view of the great house, its gardens and surrounding woods (see Walk 57). Aim towards the spire of Edensor Church to pass close to a small enclosure of trees. Just left of the churchyard a path leads down into **Edensor**.

Go left up the road which soon becomes a rough track (once a packhorse trail) ascending steadily to meet the road from Pilsley. Here there is a milestone dating from 1709. Once over the hill the road descends steeply right past Ballcross Farm and, on the left, at a sharp bend, are a gate and two signs. Follow the right-hand one, through a wood and across the golf course to reach a road near the old railway station. Descend the hill back to the start.

POINTS OF INTEREST:

Bowling Green Farm – Built in the 18th century by an owner of Haddon Hall for the entertainment of his friends. It was the pavilion to the bowling green at its front. It is possible, as you approach, to see the steps to the green and the ball-topped pillars.

Russian Cottage – Given by the Tsar Nicholas I to the 6th Duke of Devonshire (ex British Ambassador to Moscow). Built of wood with intricately carved barge boards and window surrounds.

Edensor – A model village built – in a variety of styles – about 1839 by the 6th Duke to replace the old village demolished to improve the view from Chatsworth House. The church was built about 1870 and contains fine monuments from the old church. Buried in the churchyard is Kathleen Kennedy, sister of President John Kennedy and widow of the 10th Duke's elder son.

REFRESHMENTS:
There is a café in Edensor.

Walk 70 THE NORTHERN EDGE OF KINDER SCOUT 7m (11km)

Maps: OS Sheets Landranger 110; Outdoor Leisure 1.

A wild moorland walk. Boots essential. Very rough going.

Start: At 130895, a lay-by on the south side of Snake Road near Wood Cottage.

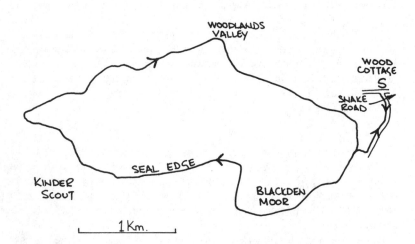

A footpath leaves the main road eastwards from the lay-by. Go over the stile and descend steeply to the River Ashop. Cross the footbridge and ascend steps up the bank to a ladder stile and open country. Follow the wall, right, to a tributary stream. The path crosses and curves right, round the shoulder of the hill into the valley of Blackden Brook. Make a note of this position as it is here that the route is rejoined on the return. The path now ascends beside Blackden Brook. Take care as it is narrow and scrambly in places, with steep drops to the brook below. Towards its head the valley narrows and steepens and it is necessary to seek a route over boulders and the rocky stream bed itself to the Kinder Scout plateau.

Turn right along the edge. The path is generally well-trodden and easy to follow with various side-trackings to avoid peat bogs. Notice the 'seal' stones, naturally

146

sculptured rocks giving the name to Seal Edge. Follow the edge path for about 2 miles until the steep valley of Fair Brook rises up to penetrate the plateau. You will recognise this not only by its steepness but by the promontory of Fairbrook Naze beyond it to the right. Descend to the headwaters of Fairbrook and follow a path on the left bank down towards the Woodlands valley. Just before you reach the River Ashop look for a wall crossing the brook. Before you reach this, ford the brook, now broad but shallow, a good place being by a sycamore tree. A path rises steeply on the opposite bank to take you above and past a sheepfold. This path climbs steeply up the hillside, but you take a small path which veers off left to follow a wall and fence. Follow this path, crossing the occasional clough, for about 1 mile to where it turns to the right into the valley of Blackden Brook. Keep following the wall/fence as it drops to cross the brook. A small path can be traced and the brook is easy to ford. Climb the opposite bank and look out for an old notice on a post giving directions to Snake Road. Go beyond the notice to join the path you started on, over the ladder stile, down to the River Ashop and back to Snake Road.

POINTS OF INTEREST:
This walk is possible because of access agreements between the National Park Authority and landowners made possible by the 1949 National Park Act following the mass trespass by ramblers on 24 April 1932.

REFRESHMENTS:
The Snake Inn, a short distance west of the start (tel no: 0433 51480).

Walk 71   **Sir William Hill and Eyam Moor**   7m (11km)
Maps: OS Sheets Landranger 119; Outdoor Leisure 24.
A hilly walk in beautiful, varied scenery with wide views.
Start: At 225780, the unmade road at the junction by Sir William
Hill.

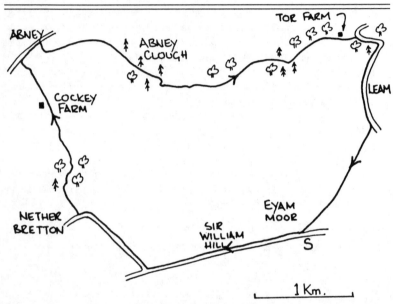

Walk up the unmade road, **Sir William Hill Road**, past the trig. point and mast for
nearly 1 mile to a road junction. A few yards on the right is a track to Nether Bretton.
There, a footpath signed 'Abney' leads down a house drive and to the right of the house.
Go diagonally across a field to another signpost, through the gateway and down by the
wall to a stile. Over this stile the path bears right to another stile, beyond which steps
lead down into **Bretton Clough**.

At a yellow arrow the path bears right (do not take the path on the right shown on
the White Peak Map) down to a footbridge over Bretton Brook. Go over a stile and
another footbridge and ascend to another stile. Follow the wall on your right through
two fields, over a ladder stile and on to the farm track to Cockey Farm. Continue ahead
part way down the wall, and on your right and round a corner, you will see a stile and

148

footpath signed 'Abney'. Go diagonally over the field towards the village, cross the farm track and continue down hill parallel to the stream to a stile. Cross the stream by footbridge and continue up the bank to the road. Turn right and go through most of the tiny farming hamlet of Abney to a footpath on the right signed 'Stoke Ford'. Continue down Abney Clough keeping to the main path, ignoring a forestry track near the bottom to the left. At Stoke Ford cross the stream over two footbridges with a gate between.

From here two paths ascend the bank, the right-hand one only being pointed. This may be taken as a short cut back to Sir William Road, branching left once out on the open moor. Our walk takes the left-hand footpath up the bank (the higher one of two). The path is easy to follow, going slightly up hill, then down after ¹/₂ mile to a stream. Here do not cross the bridge but continue over a stile, bearing up hill across an area of recent tree felling to a gate on the upper side of a larch wood. Continue through the gate to Tor Farm and up the farm track to a lane, where you turn sharp right and go up for about ¹/₂ mile past Leam Farm to Leam Hall Farm. Here a footpath on the right, signed Sir William Road, takes you 1 mile over **Eyam Moor** and back to your starting point.

POINTS OF INTEREST:

Sir William Hill Road – The road was part of the original Sheffield-Buxton turnpike, via Grindleford, abandoned in 1795 for a lower route through Eyam. The name Sir William dates back at least to 1692, referring to either Sir William Saville of Eyam Manor or Sir William Cavendish of Stoke Hall.

Bretton Clough and Eyam Moor – Traversed by several old packhorse ways, the final mile of the walk being one between Eyam and Hathersage, the stretch between Stoke Ford and Tor Farm being another.

REFRESHMENTS:

Nowhere en route but the plague village of Eyam 1 mile to the south repays a visit. Here there are several pubs including *The Prancing Pony* (tel no: 0433 31390).

Walk 72   EDALE AND JACOB'S LADDER   7½m (12km)

Maps: OS Sheets Landranger 110; Outdoor Leisure 1.

A walk that follows the first few miles of the Pennine Way.

Start: At 123855, the car park just south of Edale.

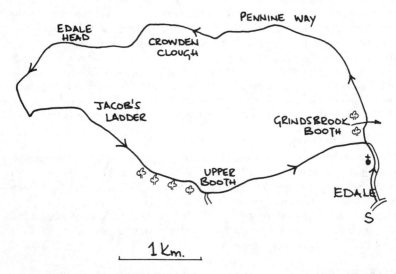

From the car park go up the lane past Edale church. Go ahead where the lane becomes a rough track and bear right at a Pennine Way sign along a narrow path through trees. Go over a footbridge, up steps and then go left on a path along Grindsbrook Clough. Go through a gate, through trees and through another gate. Go left over a stream and continue along the side of the village. The path climbs, gently at first but then more steeply. It also becomes quite rocky. Cross the stream and continue along its other side ignoring a left fork that enters a gorge. Soon you will reach high moorland from which there are superb views.

The path is obvious across the peat to the top of Crowden Clough. Here our walk leaves the Pennine Way, which turns right, and continues across a stream. Turn left and climb steeply up the side of the valley to Crowden Tower, a large gritstone outcrop. Continue along the path, crossing several groughs to pass several other gritstone outcrops including Pym Chair and the anvil-shaped Noe Stool. Here the path starts to curve left around the head of Edale going downhill to a stile and gate and a junction of paths. Turn left down the right edge of the valley to reach another path junction. Turn left here, to descend Jacob's Ladder (see Walk 91). At the bottom go over a stream and through a gate. Keep ahead now on a surfaced path, over several stiles and through several gates. Pass Lee Farm and cross a stream to reach Upper Booth. Go left through Upper Booth Farm. Go right through a gate, and follow a Public Footpath for Edale. This goes over several stiles around Grindslow Knoll. Bear left at another sign for Edale (in the middle of a field) to reach a stile by trees. Go over, turn right to another stile and go through a gate into Grindsbrook Booth. Turn right to reach the start point.

REFRESHMENTS:
The Nag's Head, Edale (tel no: 0433 70212).
The Ramblers' Inn, Edale (tel no: 0433 70268).

Walk 73   COCK HILL AND TORSIDE   7¹/₂m (12km)

Maps: OS Sheets Landranger 110; Pathfinder SK 09/19.

A good mix of moorland, valley and farmland.

Start: At 043948, the Queens pub, Old Glossop.

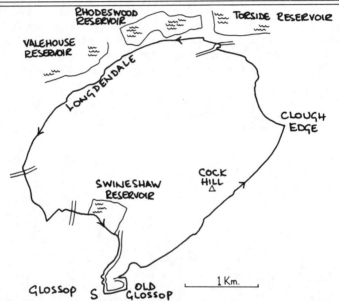

From the pub, follow Shepley Road between factories. At the bus turning circle, go left behind the factory and past three stone houses. Turn right up Charles Lane, and cross a stile left just past the last house. Follow the old packhorse trail up Cock Hill. Beyond the 'Boundary of Open Country' sign take the grassy path to the right. At a wall around the summit, cross and bear right to follow a path to a fence. Cross by the nearest stile, rejoin the path and take a right-hand fork for an obvious cleft in the hillside above. A path passes by an old slate quarry to emerge on to Glossop Moor. A series of well-maintained grouse hides marks the way, until, at a pair of ruined stone huts, the path disappears. Carry on over the brow, cross a short stretch of open moor, to the brink of Torside Clough, where a path is to be found. Go left on it along the edge of the valley.

As Torside Reservoir comes into view, a post marks where the path turns right, downhill. It leads to the maggot farm access road. Turn left along it to the road. Go right along the road over the old **Woodhead Railway** line. Leave the road immediately, by a gate on the left, to descend to the dam. Pass through the smallest of four gates, to follow a path along Rhodeswood Reservoir. As this ends, and Valehouse Reservoir begins, carry on down to a stile by a gate, and turn left along a road through a farm.

At the fork, go left over the railway bridge. Leave the road immediately by a stile, right, and follow a path through fields, crossing a stream and two walls. At a stile by a gate go over to a grassy lane. Just before the final left-hand bend into Padfield, climb a stile left and follow the wall to the far right corner of the field. Go right along the alley, then left at the end of the terrace. Cross the road and go up a lane. Go over a stile into a large field and follow the fence over several stiles on to a lane. Turn right, then left on to a grassy lane leading upwards to a tiny reservoir hiding on your right. Follow a sparse line of trees up the hill to a fence. Bear left along it to a stile leading on to the Cemetery road. Turn left on to the road, and just after it turns sharp right, cross the grass to climb a couple of steps leading over the wall. Turn right, follow the path to a gate by a stone hut, then follow a short lane past a farmhouse to the road.

Cross the road and go right to a large stile on the left. Go over and follow a low stone wall to Swineshaw Reservoir. Turn right to follow a good, high wall into a small wood, where a flight of stone steps lead down to a brook. Cross the slab bridge, and turn right on to a lane. Follow the lane through a farm and past Wall's Angling Club water. When the lane bends right, round the old hospital, carry straight on to Swineshaw Filter Station. Keep to the left of it and pass under a tall archway in some modern stone dwellings, to turn left down to the bottom of Blackshaw Road. Turn left into Wellgate, right along Wesley Street, to follow the walled brook back to the start.

POINTS OF INTEREST:

Woodhead Railway – The lines have gone now, but there are still reminders of the navvies who built the tunnels in the 1840s. The graves of several who died during the construction work can be found at St James' church, Woodhead. The Navigation pub in Hadfield is still known locally as the 'Lamp' due to its reputation as a place where lonely railway workers could find female company.

Woodhead Reservoirs – Took over 28 years to build, at a cost of £3Million. At the time of completion in 1877, they represented the largest expanse of artificial water in the world. They supply 24 million gallons of water each day for Manchester.

REFRESHMENTS:

The Queens, Old Glossop (tel no: 04574 62451).
The Wheatsheaf, Old Glossop (tel no: 04574 3046). Serves excellent food.

Walk 74 HATHERSAGE AND STANAGE EDGE $7^1/_2$m (12km)

Maps: OS Sheets Landranger 110; Pathfinder SK 28/38.

A varied walk with views over north Derbyshire. The walk along Stanage Edge follows the Derbyshire/Yorkshire border.

Start: The Oddfellows Road car park, Hathersage.

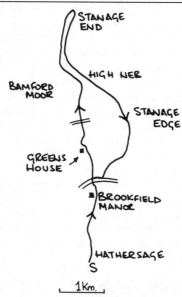

Turn left out of the car park and at the bend follow a short path to the main road opposite the Hathersage Inn. Follow Baulk Lane, immediately to the right of the inn, past the cricket ground and continue through fields. Just short of the farm the path bears left to pass behind Brookfield Manor, now a conference centre, to a gate on to Birley Lane. Cross the lane to a stile and follow the path to a small gate in the wall. Cross three fields and, after a gap in a wall, pass behind Greens House to a gate leading to a track to the right. Follow this track with the wall first on the right and then on the left until a minor road is reached at a cattle grid. Go over the grid and turn immediately right to follow a path to the right-hand end of a clump of small trees some 300 yards away. The track here is said to follow the route of the Roman road from the fort at Brough in the Hope valley to Templeborough near Rotherham.

154

A path leads from the stile towards rocks on the skyline. Follow it until it forks just before the final massive block of the Edge. Take the right fork to pass immediately under the rocks and then turn right up to join the path along the top of the Edge. Turn right along this path and follow the line of the Edge. After passing the trig. point you will reach a stile which is almost back at the Roman road crossed earlier. (Along the top look for the numbered water holes carved in the rocks and, at the top of the dip to the stile, notice the way the stones have been worn away. These stones are some distance from the track crossed earlier and raise speculation as to the actual route of the Roman road at this point.) Cross the stile and follow the wide track for a few yards left and then turn right to take the path along the Edge to reach a small rocky outcrop to the left of the path. Immediately opposite, a stone paved path winds its way down the hill to reach a small building on the road which is a Mountain Rescue Post. Go through the gate to the left of the building and join a wide track down hill to reach **North Lees Hall**.

At the hall follow the walled lane to the left and walk down the farm road to join Birley Lane at a cattle grid. Turn right along the lane and, after passing a house on the right a path leading left to the rear of Brookfields Manor is reached. Follow this, retracing the outwards path through the field and back to Hathersage.

POINTS OF INTEREST:
North Lees Hall – A National Trust property said to have been visited by the Brontes and used by Charlotte as the model for a house in *Jane Eyre*.

REFRESHMENTS:
Several in Hathersage.

Walk 75   TIDESWELL AND CRESSBROOK $7\frac{1}{2}$m (12km)

Maps: OS Sheets Landranger 119; Outdoor Leisure 24.

A walk across fine dales, including the wonderful Wye Valley.

Start: At 152955, the car park in Tideswell.

From the car park turn left, and at the memorial go right along a lane. Just before the Post Office, turn right at a Public Footpath sign. The path climbs up a series of steps to a lane. Go right along the lane for about $\frac{3}{4}$ mile to the village of **Litton**.

Go past the church to the centre of the village and there go left along the main street. At a Public Footpath sign for Wardlow go right and then left over a stile by a house. Go diagonally across a field to the bottom left-hand corner. Go over a stile and left along a walled track. At the next Public Footpath sign turn right across a field to another sign. Go left downhill to a wall corner. Go over a stile and down to the foot of Tansley Dale. Keep to the path through the dale to a stile. Go over and right to reach Cressbrook Dale. After several hundred yards , where the valley curves to the right, follow the path ahead, climbing steeply towards a wall. Do not reach it, going right instead to follow the top of the dale to a wall corner. The path drops down to cross a footbridge. On the other side it climbs again, keeping to the edge of the trees on the right, then going through woodland to reach a road. Follow this to Cressbrook, where the dale enters the valley of the River Wye. At the bottom of the hill is a footpath for Monsal Dale, Monsal Trail and Litton Mill. Go right along this, through a quarry and over a footbridge. The path now follows a bank of the Wye going through Water-cum-Jolly Dale to enter Miller's Dale.

Continue through Litton Mill to reach a Public Footpath sign for Tideswell Dale. Here go right along a wooded path through Tideswell Dale, at first on the left bank of the stream, later crossing a footbridge to follow the right bank. Go through a car park and picnic area and along a path to a road. Go along the road for 400 yards to a stile on the left just before it starts to bend left. Go over the stile to a path that goes right along the dale, climbing to join a farm track. Go right along this track back to **Tideswell.** On reaching a lane, turn right down to the road, and left into the village centre.

POINTS OF INTEREST:
Litton – A small village of beautiful 17th- and 18th-century houses grouped around a triangular green.
Tideswell – The town's large church is known as the 'Cathedral of the Peak'. It is a mainly 14th-century building with a fine pinnacled west tower. Tideswell was an important market town and lead-mining centre in the Middle Ages.

REFRESHMENTS:
Several in Tideswell and Litton.

Walk 76   **LONGSHAW LODGE**   7¹/₂m (12km)

Maps: OS Sheets Landranger 119; Outdoor Leisure 24.

A comfortable walk with no steep ascents.

Start: At 262747, the Curbar Gap car park.

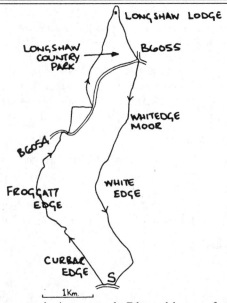

Leave the car park by the steps and gain access to the Edge path by way of a gate. Follow the obvious path along the top of **Curbar Edge** where there are serious rock climbing routes. After some distance the path drops to **Froggatt Edge**, an even more popular climbing area, and, passing between rocks, continues through a silver birch plantation to a gate and on to the Curbar to Sheffield road (B6054). Walk up the road for 100 yards and cross to a small gate leading to a stepped path to a stream. Descend and climb the other side to a stile over a fence which also has a dog flap. Follow the path along the edge of the car park, ignoring the fork down to the left, and cross over a further stile. Walk up through trees, parallel to a wall on the right. The building across the fields is the Grouse Inn. Turn right with the wall and cross over a wall stile to the road. Turning left a white gate is reached leading into the Longshaw Estate. Follow the estate road and, ultimately, after passing through a small gate you will arrive at **Longshaw Lodge**.

The return is by the estate road which goes behind the lodge to a gate on to a grassy track. Through the gate bear right past a bench and, taking the left fork, reach a road. The National Trust plaque here bears the name Wooden Pole. Cross the road junction to a stile to the left of the entry to White Lodge and follow the wire fence leading to the skyline. Follow the well-defined path, passing a National Trust map on a post, to a signpost at a gap in a wall. Continue through the gap on to White Edge and follow the path the full length of the Edge with the Wildlife Sanctuary area to the left. Shortly after passing the trig. point the path drops down to the right to a signpost at the corner of the field enclosures. The path crosses a small stream and leads back to the start of the walk via a wall stile.

If desired the walk can be shortened by using a track from near the Grouse Inn to the signpost at the gap in the wall.

POINTS OF INTEREST:

Curbar and Froggatt Edges – Very popular gritstone edges with climbs at every grade of difficulty. Climbers can be seen or heard on every reasonable day. The edges are dark millstone grit as opposed to the limestone of the other side of the Derwent Valley.

Longshaw Lodge – A National Trust property. The site of the 3-day Longshaw Sheep Dog Trials in September.

REFRESHMENTS:
The Grouse Inn (tel no: 0433 30423).

Walk 77   **AXE EDGE MOOR** $7\frac{1}{2}$m (12km)

Maps: OS Sheets Landranger 118; Outdoor Leisure 24.

An upland walk over open moorland.

Start: At 001719, opposite the Cat and Fiddle Inn.

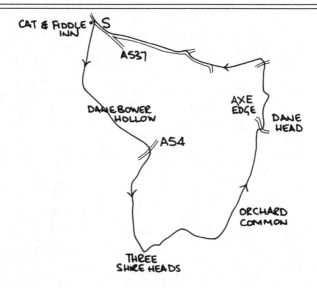

Take the track opposite the **Cat and Fiddle Inn**, signed as a Public Bridleway to Danebower. The walk goes down through Danebower Hollow rising again to reach the A54. Turn right along the road for about 100 yards and then go sharp left along a track to a gate. Go through and go right by the side of a chimney. Go downhill steeply to reach a grassy track by the River Dane. Go right along it, over a stile and, with the river to your left, go through gates and over stiles for about a mile to Three Shire Heads (see Walk 54).

    Go left over the first bridge and through a gate. Follow a stream on the right to another gate and keep on to a junction of paths. Take the uphill, tarmac track which becomes a rough track heading north across moorland. Just before the track ends, go left and up over rough moor to reach a wall corner. Go over two stiles and bear right to reach a distinct path that is followed to a road at Dane Head. Turn right then left after a few yards at a signpost for Goyt valley. Follow the grassy path Axe Edge Moor to Axe Edge. There are fine views from here. Just before an obvious brow go left along a narrower path which bears right to a road. Go over and cross moorland for a few yards to reach a path. Go left along this with a broken wall on the right, to reach a lane. Turn along the lane to a T-junction. Go left and follow the lane to the main road. Go right and back to the start.

POINTS OF INTEREST:
The Cat and Fiddle Inn – This is the second highest inn in England, at 1,690 feet, beaten only by the Tan Hill Inn to the north. It was built in the early 19th century to serve a turnpike road.

REFRESHMENTS:
The Cat and Fiddle Inn (tel no: 0298 23364).

Walk 78   CALTON LEES AND ROWSLEY   8m (13km)

Maps: OS Sheets Landranger 119; Outdoor Leisure 24.

A longer walk with varied scenery from woodland to riverside.

Start: At 258685, the Calton Lees car park.

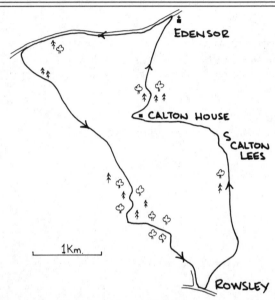

Go towards the garden centre and take the road to the right signed 'Forest Offices and Sawmill'. At a road junction go through the middle of three gates to a track past a large oak tree. After ³/₄ mile the track passes through Calton Houses, and doubles back to go between houses into a lane. Go to the right and through a gate, keeping to the wall on the right. At the third power line pole turn left towards a barn and lodge. Go through the gate to the left of the barn, down a track through trees and over a stile into a field. Go towards two pine plantations and follow a path to the left of the right-hand plantation, towards Edensor church, and pass to the right of it to the road. Turn left and, after 400 yards, left again through gates. Continue up Edensor village street (see Walk 69) past the Lodge.

Go up the track signed 'Unfit for Motor Vehicles'. After 1 mile turn left at a road junction. In the field to the right is an interesting old road. After ¹/₂ mile on the left is

162

a footpath signed 'Rowsley 3m'. Go through a gate and over a stile to the top of the rise where the road forks. Turn right and go around the pine trees to the junction of three paths. Take the path straight ahead, towards the dip. At the field take a path to the right, towards the pond. Follow the fence to the right of the pond to a gate. Take the path leading towards the three power line poles on the horizon. The path turns left to a gate in a wire fence. Go over a stile by the gate and head towards the trees. Pass the tumuli, right, and head for a stile on the right. Go over and straight ahead with the wall on the right. Go over the broken down wall and turn left. After 300 yards (after passing under the power lines) turn right into trees and on to a gap in a wall. Turn left and follow the wall. After 100 yards go down through the pine trees and turn right at a junction. At the next junction turn right and go to the bottom of the track. Go through the second gate on the left and along the lane, with the hedge to the left. At the junction take the track ahead. After $^1/_2$ mile go through the gate and down the track ahead. At the end of the track join a road between buildings, go down hill past the church, and turn left on to the marked path. Go under the railway arch. If refreshments are required at this point go over the river into the village to the pub.

Carry straight on, following the river. At the second gate go left along the edge of a field, through a gate and continue over the field to the right, towards the end of the line of trees. Turn right at the end of the trees and after 150 yards head left diagonally to a gate in the wall. Go under the power lines to the gate opposite. Go through the gate and diagonally left towards the large tree. Go over a stile and turn right along the line of the wall to the farmyard. Go round left to a stile and over it on to a lane. Turn right and follow the lane to the start point.

Walk 79   **GRINAH STONES**   8m (13km)

Maps: OS Sheets Landranger 110; Outdoor Leisure 1.

A walk to the heart of Bleaklow. It includes some rough, off-track walking.

Start: At 168939, Kings Tree at the head of Howden Reservoir.

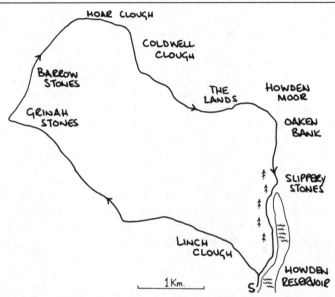

Pass through the gate at Kings Tree and, after crossing the ford, take the grassy track to the left rising through the trees to a wall. Beyond the wall take the track rising steeply up the hillside following the line of an old ditch. At the top, keep left along the brow of Linch Clough crossing a broken wall and following the track along the join of heather and grass. The path crosses a short stretch of heather and skirts the edge of a large hollow with a stream in the bottom. You cross a small stream and swing right to another stream. Cross the stream at a small waterfall and bear slightly left to a clough or old drainage ditch. (This is the middle of the three which join to form Linch Clough). The clough starts small but soon widens and has a very narrow stream wandering in the bottom. Follow the course of the clough on the right-hand side using a narrow path through the heather. To the right at about 300 yards distance can be seen the marker post for a rain gauge. As the ground levels off the path follows the line of the main drainage ditch to the right towards Grinah Stones, which can soon be seen in the distance. You pass the end of a new deep ditch which runs away right and, where the old broad ditch ends, continue on a less distinct track slightly right towards Grinah Stones. As the track curves right towards Round Hill continue directly ahead to descend a small clough, cross a stream and climb up the hillside to the rocks of **Grinah Stones.**

The path along the top of the slope just climbed leads from Grinah Stones to Barrow Stones to the right. From Barrow Stones descend the slope very slightly right to reach the Derwent where the stream down Barrow Clough joins. There is no defined path but descending from the Barrow Stones in this direction can lead only to the Derwent so wandering a little from the line is not important. Any water encountered now will ultimately enter Howden Reservoir so every stream is a direction indicator. Reaching the river find a crossing place and join the path on the other side. Follow this path to the right (downstream) making occasional detours around marshy areas and passing the bottom of Hoar Clough to reach a place where the valley narrows at Coldwell Clough. This place is also marked by a ruined sheepfold on the other bank of the Derwent. Follow the path along the Derwent until the valley broadens and the path rises left to pass a tree. Cross a stretch of level wet ground. A short path now leads to a shelter at Lands Clough from where a broad track leads down the valley to the packhorse bridge across the river at Slippery Stones. Cross the bridge and follow the road through the trees to pass the bottom of Linch Clough at the ford and arrive back at the starting point.

POINTS OF INTEREST:
Grinah Stones – These rocks, together with Bleaklow Stones, can be said to be the heart of Bleaklow.

REFRESHMENTS:
There are none other than the *snack bar at Fairholme* so take food and drink with you if it is likely to be needed.

Walk 80　　STONY MIDDLETON AND EYAM　　8m (13km)

Maps: OS Sheets Landranger 119; Pathfinder SK 27/37.

A rugged walk in varied terrain.

Start: At 229754, the small car park opposite the limestone cliffs, café and climbing shop on the A623.

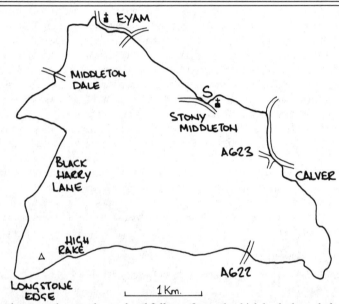

From the car park cross the road and follow a footpath which leads through the cliffs and narrows as it climbs through the woodland giving quite a sharp drop on the left. This is a very popular area for climbers. Continue to **Eyam.** Walk along the main road and turn left along New Close. Climb the hill to a junction and go left for a few yards. Go over a stile opposite and head right to a second stile. Go over and follow a route down to the right-hand corner of the next field where steps give access to a narrow path which eventually takes you in to Middleton Dale. Cross over the road, Dale Brook and head up the wooded lane by the quarries. At the junction go left up a hill to superb views of Eyam and Froggatt and Curbar Edges.

At the first turn right proceed along a farm track, passing High Fields to the left, down in to Coombes Dale. Go over stiles continuing along a wall uphill to the junction of Longstone Edge and High Rake. Here the route goes left along High Rake. This gravel track reaches a high point with spectacular views. The remains of deep quarries can be seen on both sides of the track, now exhausted of minerals by the opencast works. The track descends, quite steeply at times, to the A622. Cross over to a track to Bramley Farm. Descend into the valley a short distance past the farm to a stile on the left. Go over to a path through two fields with a wood and the river Derwent on the right. The path goes through three fields away from the river and into Calver. From Calver crossroads walk along the A622 and after a short distance a footpath on the left is followed for about $^1/_2$ mile, passing Stony Middleton Hall, back to the start.

POINTS OF INTEREST:
Eyam – A historical village with many memories of 17th-century plague. Also worth seeing are the church and the infamous stocks.

REFRESHMENTS:
There are numerous pubs and cafés in the villages of Calver, Eyam and Stony Middleton.

Walk 81 ROCKING STONES AND HOWDEN CLOUGH 8m (13km)

Maps: OS Sheets Landranger 110; Outdoor Leisure 1.

An airy walk along part of the Eastern Edges. A steady ascent in the early stages and a short steep stretch of rough ground.

Start: At 168939, Kings Tree at the head of Howden Reservoir.

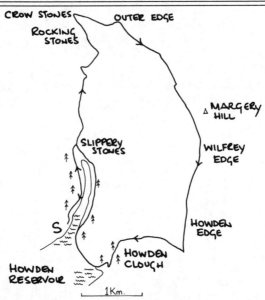

Leave Kings Tree by the gate and follow the track across the ford and continue along parallel to the river to the packhorse bridge at **Slippery Stones**. Cross the bridge and at the other side stand to look left. The first objective of the walk is Crow Stones Edge which can be seen above the sheepfold on the skyline. Continue left to cross a wooden footbridge and then turn right to a fork. Follow the main track to the left passing a National Trust sign for 'Howden Moor'. Take a rutted grassy path slanting right up the hillside, following a wire fence. Cross a small footbridge and reach a stile in the fence. Here a path joins from the left and a narrow path leads off to the right. Follow this path round the shoulder of the hill to a ruined cabin. Now head for a stake which can be seen on the hill above. This is a marker stake for a shooting butt and is on a track which leads along the Edge. There is no well-marked path to the stake but as consolation you may start a hare. Reach the path at the stake and follow it left towards Crow Stones rising gradually to a level stretch along the Edge. The track is fairly well marked and is joined by a path coming from Outer Edge which can be seen on the right. Continue along the track to **Rocking Stones.**

From the Rocking Stones a faint path leads in a direct line to Outer Edge crossing some channels in the peat on the way. The track can be lost in these channels but with the rocks of the Edge in view at all times there is no problem. Reaching the top of the rocks a line of stakes can be seen marking a wide path leading to the trig point to the right. This path, as do most of the others on the high ground of the Eastern Edges, forms part of the 40 mile Derwent Watershed Walk. Follow the path until, just as the land starts to rise from Margery Hill, the Cut Gate path is reached at a cairn. Turn right and just before a post is reached at the brow of the hill take the path to the left to skirt Margery Hill and continue towards Wilfrey Edge.

At the high point on the edge the path follows the line of an old drainage ditch in the direction of Back Tor, seen on the skyline beyond the deep groove forming Abbey Brook. Follow the path along the ditch, losing height, until, almost on the edge of Abbey Brook, the remains of a wall are reached. Follow this wall steeply down to the right towards Howden Clough (the valley to the right with a clump of conifers in the bottom and scattered small trees on the hillside). There is a break of some 70 yards in the remnants of the wall where the track crosses a boggy hollow: this can be avoided by swinging right above the gap and keeping to the tussocky grass whilst circling the bad patch to rejoin the wall. Follow the path through Howden Clough and join a forest track running down to the road along the side of Howden Reservoir. Turn right along the road and walk to Slippery Stones where the Derwent is re-crossed and the early part of the walk retraced back to Kings Tree.

POINTS OF INTEREST:

Slippery Stones Bridge – Was originally sited in the village of Derwent several miles downstream. It was dismantled when the valley was flooded to form the reservoir and re-erected on this spot. See the stone in the left-hand parapet of the bridge.

Rocking Stones – Good examples of weather-sculpted rock. The Holme Moss TV mast dominates the view which includes Yorkshire, Bleaklow and Kinder.

Maps: OS Sheets Landranger 119; Outdoor Leisure 24.
Easy going, mostly on disused railways, tracks and lanes.
Start: At 128604, the square in the centre of Hartington.

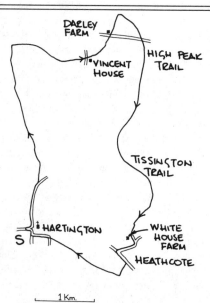

DARLEY FARM

HIGH PEAK TRAIL

VINCENT HOUSE

TISSINGTON TRAIL

HARTINGTON

S

WHITE HOUSE FARM

HEATHCOTE

1 Km.

Take the road from the square uphill towards the church, turn left and continue up the lane for about ¹/₂ mile. Looking back you can see the Hartington Stilton Cheese factory. Watch for a footpath sign on the left on the far side of Horse Croft as the lane bends to the right. The next stretch of the walk northwards is marked at stiles with yellow arrows. Head diagonally over a field to a stile to the left of a gateway. Continue through the next two fields going over stiles. Bear left through a gate on to a track then go through another gate as track bends sharp left. Follow the wall on the right until it ends, go ahead and the ground levels then gradually bear left downhill over rocky hillside and you reach a stile. Go over to a path going diagonally over the field uphill towards a ruin. Pass the ruin on the lower side and bear right uphill over a limestone rock outcrop. Continue uphill bearing right past two field corners, cross a farm track, go over a stile and follow a wall down to the valley bottom. Turn right over a step stile and walk in a straight line up the valley to a pond. Continue via stiles straight across two fields, then bear left up the hill and down to a lane and farm (Vincent House). Go straight through the farmyard, then up the hill on the right-hand of two farm tracks (the footpath has been diverted from the left-hand track). At the end of the track follow the wall, left, and yellow arrows through five fields to Darley Farm, where a stile directly over the road leads through the farmyard. Go through the gate ahead and walk up on the left of a wall to the steps on to the **High Peak Trail.**

Turn right along the trail to Parsley Hay Picnic Site. Shortly after this the trail divides. Take the right fork, the Tissington Trail (see Walk 4), through a deep cutting. Continue along the Trail for about $1\frac{1}{2}$ miles. After a bridge over a road continue to the far end of picnic site at the former **Hartington Station**, where you take a footpath to the right signed to Heathcote. This goes between walls then over a stile. Continue with the wall on your left through four fields to a track. Turn left at Whitehouse Farm, right at the road, sharp left at Heathcote Mere, right up a track and right at the T-junction. Turn left when the track meets the road near the **Youth Hostel**, to return to the start.

POINTS OF INTEREST:
High Peak Trail – Former Cromford and High Peak Railway connecting the Cromford and Peak Forest Canals. The only railway to be built (by a canal engineer) like a canal with long levels and steep inclines and stations called wharfs (eg at Parsley Hay) and one of the earliest lines in the country, opening in 1830.
Hartington Station – The old signal box is now an information office, open in summer, containing old equipment and photographs.
Youth Hostel – Formerly Hartington Hall and dated 1611.

REFRESHMENTS:
A number of refreshment opportunities in Hartington.

Maps: OS Sheets Landranger 110; Outdoor Leisure 1.

An easy to follow walk on lanes and moorland tracks with spectacular views.

Start: At 0798819, at the junction of the 'yellow' and 'white' roads at Slackhall just off the A625.

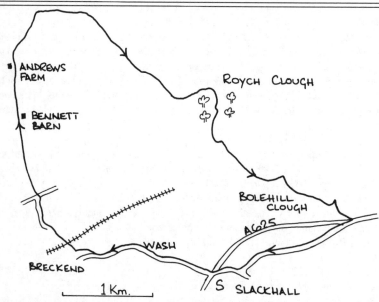

Walk down to the main road, A625, cross it and continue opposite taking the left-hand road uphill, passing the entrance to the **Chestnut Centre**. Continue on this road to Wash. Once through the village look for a signed footpath on the right. Follow this over a lane, through a small gate opposite, up to a bridge over the railway, and on to Breckhead. Here turn left to reach a road, and right along it, past Gorstey Low Farm to a T-junction. Go straight across up a track.

After about $\frac{1}{2}$ mile, past Dewshap Farm, the track goes to the left of Bennett Barn and continues as a path up to a gate and stile by the wall on the left. Go over on to a green lane to Bullhill. Here after emerging on to a farm track the green lane leads to a gate. Follow the wall to Andrews Farm. Just past the farm you reach a crossroads of tracks.

Here turn right along the wall, over a stile and on up to the Access Point (see Walk 70) over a stile on to a bridleway.

Turn right on the bridleway. Continue past a footpath on the left signed for Edale and Hayfield and on down to a gate and stile marking your exit from the Access Land. Where the path forks at two gates, go through the left-hand one, down to the fords at Roych Clough. Then as you climb up again, just before the trees, you are over the railway tunnel. After another $^1/_2$ mile you cross Bolehill Clough, the stream which flows down through the Chestnut Centre. Shortly after crossing the next stream you reach the main road (A625). Turn right along the road to a gate and stile on the left. Keep to the right-hand track which changes to a green lane. Go straight ahead at the barn, back to your starting point.

POINTS OF INTEREST:

Chestnut Centre – An otter and owl haven open to the public 10.30am–5.30pm daily.

Walk 84   **AROUND ELTON**   9m (14.5km)

Maps: OS Sheets Landranger 119; Outdoor Leisure 24.

A walk across moorlands and along a quiet river dale.

Start: At 237603, opposite the Miners Standard in Winster.

From the Miners Standard walk uphill, turning right along the minor road to a rough track on the right signed 'Limestone Way'. The way ahead, through to Harthill Moor, is that of the Old Portway (see 'Alport' below). Follow the track, now known as Islington Lane (Islington is a lost village) to a road. Cross over on the same track (now Dudwood Lane) which is now metalled. Where it reaches the main road go ahead via a stile up the path to Robin Hood's Stride (left) and Cratcliff Rocks (right). In these rocks, by a yew tree, is a small hermitage with a 4ft high carved crucifix, both of unknown antiquity. Beyond the Stride cross a stile and then walk diagonally across fields to a narrow lane at **Harthill Moor** Farm drive. Turn right following the lane and walk downhill all the way to the bridge at Alport (see Walk 31). Go over the bridge and turn along the village street. At the main road, cross the bridge and turn left into Bradford Dale and follow the path upstream to a road. (A diversion to Youlgreave can

174

be taken by crossing the packhorse bridge part way along the path.) Take the Elton road for about 250 yards before turning left along Mawstone Farm drive with the remains of Mawstone Mine on the left. Pass through the farm to a track going left around the wood opposite. At the end of the track continue ahead on a path following a fairly straight line across fields, passing a narrow row of trees and further fields towards Anthony Hill. The path goes to the right of the hill and reaches a road. Turn down the road to a stile at the end of the first field on the left. Go over and head for the top-left corner of the second field to exit via a gate to the road near the church in **Elton**.

Take the road opposite the church and at a fork go left to a T-junction. Continue ahead along a farm track to a stile to the end of the fourth field past the farm. The way ahead is rarely walked so there are no path signs. Go over the stile and another in the top-left corner of the field. Maintain the same line across more fields to a field corner with a small reservoir in the opposite left corner. Look ahead to the road and its junction with a minor road coming in from the right. Take a straight line across the remaining fields to exit on to the road via a gate. Turn left along the road and walk back to the start of the walk.

POINTS OF INTEREST:

Harthill Moor – To the right of the field path is an earthwork, a standing stone and a small stone circle – all associated with the activities of pre-historic man. Adjacent to the farm is an Iron Age fort known as 'Castle Ring'.

Elton – From the Saxon 'Ell's Tun' (farmstead) situated to be near the Old Portway. Once a lead mining village.

REFRESHMENTS:
The Bulls Head , Youlgreave (tel no: 0629 636307).

Walk 85   **HOPE AND CASTLETON**   9m (14.5km)

Maps: OS Sheets Landranger 110; Outdoor Leisure 1.

A moderately difficult walk over some of the finest hills in the Peak District.

Start: At 173835, the church in Hope.

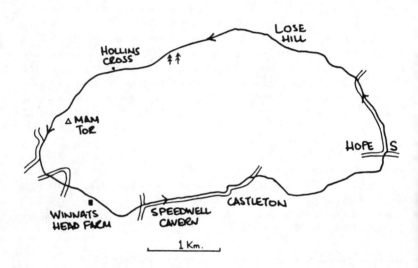

From the church the Edale road is followed for about ¹/₄ mile to a lane with a sign for Moorgate Guest House. Follow the left fork and after a very short distance go left through a gate across a lane and immediately right along a rocky path. Go through a small gate and follow a path along the slope of Lose Hill. A short deviation from the path to the summit is well worth it for the fine spectacular views of the northern Peak. From it one can see the Kinder Scout plateau to the north and Win Hill in the east. The well-marked path continues towards Mam Tor, Back Tor Wood and Hollins Cross (see Walk 50). From here fork left to the top of Mam Tor (see Walk 50), another superb vantage point. It is possible from here to pick out the route back to Hope.

    The track follows the cliff edge and goes down to the road at Mam Nick. Go over a stile, crossing the road to a gate and then follow the left path at a disused quarry. The path reaches another road which leads to Winnats Pass, a spectacular, steep gorge where, to the left, the **Blue John** and Treak Cliff Caverns are located, as are the underground waterways of **Speedwell Mine**. Follow the road down into Castleton. Go through the village and after the last buildings a footpath on the right follows the banks of Peakhole Water for a further $2^1/_2$ miles back to Hope.

POINTS OF INTEREST:

Blue John Cavern – World famous source of Blue John stone – open every day 9.30am–6.00pm (10.00am till dusk in winter). Refreshments available and extensive gift shop (tel no: 0433 20638).

Speedwell Mine – A disused lead mine, visited by boat. 840 ft below the surface is the world famous Bottomless Pit which once swallowed 40,000 tons of rubble without any effect on the water level. Open daily throughout the year. Sweets, ice-cream and drinks available (tel no: 0433 20512).

REFRESHMENTS:

Numerous in Castleton.

WINDGATHER ROCKS 9m (14.5km)

Maps: OS Sheets Landranger 119; Outdoor Leisure 24.

High level walking over moorland along an ancient ridgeway track.

Start: At 012748, the car park at Errwood Hall.

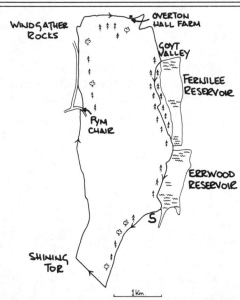

From the south end of the car park ascend the hill on a path to a ladder stile. Cross to the boundary wall and follow it left for approximately $\frac{1}{2}$ mile to another ladder stile and a clear path on the right. Follow this path to the wall corner. The route from here to Windgather Rocks is an ancient ridgeway track. Keeping the wall on your left follow the path to the road at Pym Chair (a chair-shaped stone inscribed PC, now destroyed). Turn right on the road and, shortly, left over two stiles heading slightly left to another stile by the roadside wall. Follow the concession path just inside the wall, with Goyt forest on the right, and cross a stile to Windgather Rocks.

A short way along the rocks turn right and cross a stile to reach the edge of a wood. Turn left along a fenced path by the wood side. Cross the stile at the end of the path to reach another path which cuts across the corner of the wood to a ladder stile. Follow the path line parallel to the wood to reach a road and a cattle grid. Go over on to a farm track and follow this past Overton Hall Farm, to where it curves left to meet another track acutely right. Turn up this track, pass through a gate and walk past Madscar Farm. Turn left via a second gate to Knipe Farm where the track turns right. Continue ahead to a metalled path at the end of Fernilee Reservoir. Follow this path over a stile and through trees in the direction of a footpath signed 'Errwood Dam'. After a short distance the path goes right to cross a footbridge and then continues through trees descending to the road by the dam. Take the road along the reservoir back to **Errwood Hall** and the start of the walk.

POINTS OF INTEREST:

Errwood Hall – Now a ruin, it was a 19th-century Italian-styled building built by Samuel Grimshawe. A small shrine and cemetery still remain and rhododendrons abound.

Walk 87   MONSAL HEAD AND MONSAL DALE   9m (14.5km)

Maps: OS Sheets Landranger 119; Outdoor Leisure 24.

Easy walking after a steepish climb. Many fine views particularly from Monsal Head.

Start: At 220707, the car park by the bridge, Bakewell.

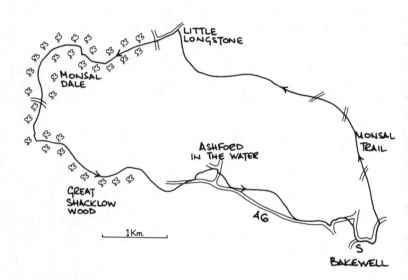

Leave the car park to the left along a minor road and turn right at the junction to walk up the hill to the old railway station. Take the **Monsal Trail** left from the station passing, after about $1^1/_4$ miles, the old **Hassop Station** and, later, that of Great Longstone. Shortly after passing through a cutting a footpath from Ashford to Little Longstone crosses your path. Follow this to the right across the fields to Little Longstone. On reaching a road turn left to **Monsal Head**.

    Pass in front of the hotel to a stile. Go over and take a descending path through the trees on the side of Fin Cop (around by an Iron Age hill fort) to the river Wye and Monsal Dale. Follow the river downstream crossing a stile and going over a small stream and a field to reach the main road at a car park. In the car park go left a few yards before turning right up the bank to a stile. Go over and follow Path Number 3 which

180

climbs steeply to Great Shacklow Wood. A path goes through the wood descending at the far side to pass an old bobbin mill with twin water-wheels. Go over a stile and across fields to the Sheldon Road. Turn left and then right along the A6 and left again over **Sheepwash Bridge** into Ashford.

Walk down the street and turn right at the Devonshire Arms to reach a T-junction. Cross to the old, now unused road which goes over the river by a bridge inscribed '**M Hyde 1664**'. Just beyond the bridge turn left on to a metalled path to and through a kissing gate. A path crosses the field climbing the hillside, then continues close to the river over three stiles and curves right to pass between houses to a road. Cross the road and continue along a similar path with a stile at the end and go ahead to reach a gate and the A6. Turn left for $^1/_2$ mile, nearing a right-hand bend where you turn left over a 17th-century packhorse bridge. After 250 yards, cross the wall into water meadows following a path back to the river bridge and car park in Bakewell.

POINTS OF INTEREST:

Monsal Trail – Lies along the bed of the old LMS railway from Bakewell to Buxton.
Hassop Station – Was built at the request of the Duke of Devonshire to serve Chatsworth House, 4 miles away.
Monsal Head – Offers a magnificent viewpoint overlooking the Monsal and Cressbrook Dales and the old railway viaduct.
Sheepwash Bridge – Where the sheep were collected in an adjacent stone fold and washed in the river.
M Hyde 1664 – This packhorse bridge was where he lost his life when his horse jumped off the bridge into the river.

REFRESHMENTS:
The Monsal Head Hotel (tel no: 062 987 250).
Many available in Bakewell.

Walk 88   LADYBOWER AND DERWENT EDGE   9m (14.5km)

Maps: OS Sheets Landranger 110; Outdoor Leisure 1.

A walk memorable for the views over the north Derbyshire. The first mile includes some fairly steep paths.

Start: At 195865, the car park at Ladybower Reservoir.

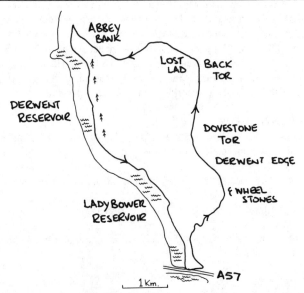

Walk up the water board road to the east of the viaduct carrying the A57 over the reservoir. Turn sharp right before the gate and continue behind the houses until the track ends at a gate. Do not use this gate but use the one on the left to reach a track which leads up through trees. Follow the line of the power lines until the trees end. Follow the path uphill, passing under the power lines, towards the rocks of Whinstone Lee Tor but, before reaching them, climb the hill to a notch in the Edge and join the path along the top. At a junction follow the left path. Shortly after a path crossing is reached signed 'Moscar-Derwent', with a shooting butt on the right. Go ahead, passing Wheel Stones, on the right, Salt Cellar, Dovestone Tor and Cakes of Bread until a further sign is reached for Abbey Grange-Strines. Again walk ahead to reach Back Tor with its trig. point. (The path occasionally splits to avoid bad patches.)

182

Pass to the left of Back Tor to follow the path across wet ground to the Lost Lad with its cairn and plinth with engraved topograph. Follow the path roughly north-west keeping left at a fork and continue to bear left to a shallow gully leading down the hill. At the foot of this follow the track which starts half left, swings right to the gully and finally leads off half left again. Follow the green track, rutted by the tyres of shooters' vehicles, across fairly level ground and over a broken wall. Leave it to go right to a stile over a fence. Take the path indicated on the signpost to Derwent Reservoir which can soon be seen below. At a further signpost turn right along the track and follow the line of the broken wall until it dips to a signpost, in a hollow, for Abbey Grange-Strines. Follow the arrow to Abbey Grange and, after an opening in a wall, walk down through the trees to join a road along the reservoir. Follow this to pass the end of the **Derwent Dam** with its access to Fairholmes Picnic Area. Pass through Derwent and Mill Brook, where there is a map of the submerged village, to the start of the Derwent-Moscar path crossed earlier. Keep to the reservoir side until a gate is reached. Go through to the starting point.

POINTS OF INTEREST:

Derwent Dam – The site of an annual fly-past by aircraft of World War II. The dam was used by the RAF to train for low-level attack on the dams in the Ruhr because of its resemblance to the German dams with their two towers. The sight of a Lancaster bomber flying at very low level over the water is certainly impressive.

Walk 89　　　**ALPORT CASTLES**　　　9m (14.5km)

Maps: OS Sheets Landranger 110; Outdoor Leisure 1.

Good visibility is needed to help route-finding. One short steep section.

Start: At 154927, where the River Westend enters Howden Reservoir.

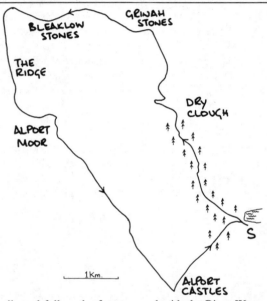

Cross the stile and follow the forestry road with the River Westend on the right. Continue, passing a steep track coming down from the left which is the return route, to a clearing with a bridge over the river. Cross the bridge and follow the track through conifers and up the hillside in zig-zags. At the top Bleaklow Stones and Grinah Stones come into view as the path passes a wire enclosure on the right. The path leads off between peat banks passing a new ditch leading off to the right and continues in the same line beyond the turning area though it is less distinct. Pass the end of an old wide drainage ditch to join a path leading left towards Grinah Stones. Where the path swings right towards Round Hill a path goes left to follow a small clough and over a stream directly to Grinah Stones (see Walk 79).

184

Take the path which curves around one of the upper branches of the River Westend crossing a number of small streams to Bleaklow Stones. The path forks a number of times and in each case the right fork should be taken to lead up the slope to the stones. The view from Bleaklow Stones includes the whole of the Bleaklow and Kinder area, Holme Moss and Black Hill, South Yorkshire with Emley Moor TV mast and the eastern edges of the Derwent Valley. From the rocks the general direction is Kinder Plateau, the ridge to be followed starting slightly to the right. A path can vaguely be seen along the top. Take this until the land drops away and the path bends left to drop to a dip between a branch of the River Westend and Alport Dale. The path then rises and bears left, becomes narrower and rises to the right again to cross the brow. The path is fairly well-defined to the trig. point ahead but crosses an area of wet rough ground which calls for some minor detours. From the trig. point the path drops gently to the edge of Alport Dale and continues along this to a wall on the right at Birchin Hat where a broken wall joins from the left. Cross this wall with **Alport Castles** dropping away to the right and walk sharp left to follow the path downhill to pass a shelter and enter trees through a gap in the wall. The track steepens and joins a forestry road. Turn right and return to the starting point of the walk.

POINTS OF INTEREST:
Alport Castles – The site of an ancient landslip, the Castles being the detached mass of the slip.

REFRESHMENTS:
There is a snack bar at Fairholme.

Walk 90   MAM TOR AND RUSHUP EDGE   9m (14.5km)

Maps: OS Sheets Landranger 110; Pathfinder SK 08/18.

A fine ridge walk around the Vale of Edale, starting with a stiff climb.

Start: At 124853, the car park near the bottom of the lane to Edale.

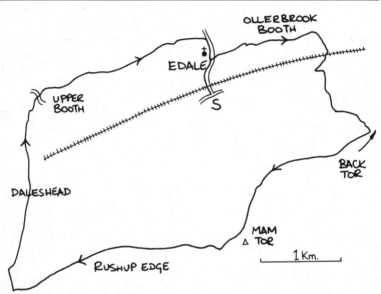

Leave the car park by the toilets, turning right to walk under the railway bridge and up the lane into **Edale**. Turn right just before the graveyard, down a stony lane which opens out and passes through Ollerbrook Booth. At Cotefield farm, take a right fork across a field to a gate. Go through, bear right and cross a brook. After a stile the path joins a narrow lane leading down to the main road. Turn right, follow the road under the railway and then take the first left, down a lane over the river to a farm. Cross a stile by the gate and follow a stony track uphill to another stile. Ignoring the well-defined path ahead, follow the wall, left. Where it turns left, follow the path, right, between hummocks. Beyond a stile in a wall, the path becomes faint, as it leads up to the right of the cliffs of Back Tor. On reaching the ridge take the rocky path to the summit of Back Tor. Retrace your steps and follow the path via Hollins Cross to Mam Tor.

From the trig. point on Mam Tor (see Walk 50), follow the National Trust's stone path to a road. Go over a stile at either end of the high wall opposite and take a path on to Rushup Edge. Beyond the high point of the ridge, look ahead and right, for a railway tunnel air-shaft, which gives its name to Toot Hill, through which it rises. Shortly, just as the path becomes enclosed between steep banks, a signpost indicates a path right, towards Barber Booth. Follow it until a tall post is reached. Bear right and descend to pass another signpost. Look for a faint path on your left by a small cairn, leading steeply downhill. Take this and at the bottom, cross a brook and two stiles and head diagonally across a field to another stile. Cross the next field and head, via stile and a gate, for the National Trust's Dalehead Information Shelter. Turn right along the front of the buildings and left between them to cross the brook. The path leads past another air-shaft and around the hillside above a farmhouse where it disappears. Head across the fields for a wall leading to a barn. Go through a gate, go round the barn and across a field towards the back of a farmhouse. Go through a small gate and over a stile. Bear left, heading for the nearest trees. The path becomes clearer and leads over a stile beneath a large tree, then crosses the river by a narrow bridge and heads uphill to Upper Booth.

Cross the road by the telephone box and carry on through the farmyard, until a signpost for Edale sends you right over a stile by a gate. Turn left, then right along the track towards Grindsbrook Booth. When the track disappears, bear left uphill until it re-appears. Climb a stile and follow the path up behind a grassy knoll. The path goes downhill over stiles until a signpost sends you left across a field to a stile. Go over this, turn right to follow the brook to a road opposite the Nag's Head, Edale. Turn right to follow the lane to the start.

POINTS OF INTEREST:
Edale – Popular walking centre whose population of 300–400 trebles in summer. Since 1965 it has been the start/end point of the Pennine Way.

REFRESHMENTS:
The Nag's Head, Edale (tel no: 0433 70212), a café in a railway carriage.
The Rambler's Inn, Edale (tel no: 0433 70268).

Walk 91   KINDER SCOUT AND MOUNT FAMINE   9m (14.5km)

Maps: OS Sheets Landranger 110; Pathfinder SK 08/18.

A stiff climb to a high level route. Should not be attempted by the inexperienced in bad weather.

Start: At 048869, the Quarry, on the road from Hayfield to Kinder Reservoir.

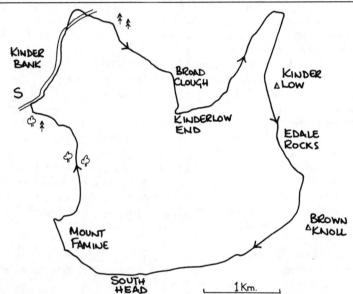

From the quarry car park follow the main road up the valley. At the gate leading on to Water Authority land turn right to cross the River Sett. Follow the lane until it bends right. Bear left through a gate and along the river bank. At a path junction go right, uphill. Cross a narrow lane, to follow a stony track. Go through a gateway in the corner of the field, turn right and up, passing through another gate. When the fence turns right, go straight on over the brow and as the trail disappears, go between two gateposts in a dilapidated wall. Head for the far end of the long wall to your right and cross a short open stretch to a gate. Go through, turn right and follow a track between walls. When the left wall end and the right wall turns right, go half left and up to a good path through the rocks of Kinder Low End.

The path climbs, then flattens out, turns right (as Kinder Downfall is seen) and climbs again. Now look out for a right fork to the summit. At the top, turn right along one of many paths near the Edge. Be sure to turn inland if your path starts to drop. Pass the trig. point and keep left of the fenced area of the Kinder Re-vegetation Experiment. About half-way along the fence turn left and head for a large rocky outcrop. Turn right here, crossing a short stretch of open moor, to join a good rocky trail. Follow it around a bend then left and downward to a wide track. Here, sympathise with those who have climbed **Jacob's Ladder** to your left! If it is raining, turn right to return to Hayfield, in which case you'll find **Edale Cross** hiding behind a wall on your right.

Our route is straight ahead up Brown Knoll, following the wall, several stiles, but be sure to be on the right of the fence when it ends. Follow the wall right, then left. Follow the wall all the way to the base of South Head and join the path from Rushup Edge. The track passes to the right of South Head, between two impressive, but pointless, stone gateposts and, through a gate round the back of Mount Famine. Go through a gate to a lane. At the bottom of a long straight stretch, before a collection of corrugated sheds, turn right through a gate into a field. Follow the wall, left, until the path becomes clearer. Go through a gate on the brow of the hill. Ignore two right-hand forks and as soon as you reach the road, leave it immediately to the left. After a short rise the path levels and passes through a gate. Take the more inviting of the two paths below the woods, to pass behind a farmhouse. Beyond the wall is replaced by a fence. When the wall reappears, cross it by stile and descend an imposing stone staircase to the campsite. Pass through two gates, turn right before a bridge and follow the camp access road back to the quarry.

POINTS OF INTEREST:

Jacob's Ladder – Starting at the old packhorse bridge, the original steps on this steep path were cut by one Jacob Marshall, a resident of Edale Head House in the 17th century.

Edale Cross – One of the stone crosses that marked the boundary of the Royal Forest of the Peak, a strictly protected hunting reserve.

REFRESHMENTS:

The Royal Hotel, Hayfield (tel no: 0663 42721).

Maps: OS Sheets Landranger 110; Pathfinder SK 09/19.
A moderate walk along the Longdendale Valley.
Start: At 015973, Arnfield Reservoir Dam.

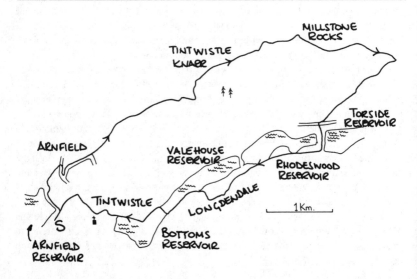

Walk up the narrow lane between the reservoir and the end of the terraced row of houses. At the end of the stone wall on your left go past a gate to a turnstile which leads to a field. Follow the field's left edge along the reservoir. Beyond another turnstile, the path leads on to the lane to Arnfield Farm. At the farm, turn right and follow the road downhill, over a bridge, and uphill to a sharp left turn. Doubling back, pass the farm and cross a stile. A good track now climbs the valley of Arnfield Brook emerging on to Tintwistle (pronounced 'tinsel') Low Moor, before climbing to Tintwistle Knarr. At the top of the climb, pass to the right of a tall post, to follow a fence on your right. At a stile at Rawkins Brook turn left on a path signed for Crowden via Lads Leap. The path becomes faint as it climbs to Millstone Rocks. Turn right at the top, on to a better path along the edge of the moor to Lads Leap at Hollins Clough. From here the path follows the brook upstream a little way, crosses to turn back down the other side and, shortly, bears left to cross a boggy moor, following a line of cairns. At a wall bear to the left of it and follow it down towards the bottom of the Crowden Valley. At a small wood turn right over a large ladder stile.

Turn right again immediately to follow the wall up the hillside. A grassy path follows a line of posts around the hill, then over a stile towards a stone barn. Pass below the barn on a small section of the the Pennine Way. Beyond a gate, the path descends to emerge, through another gate by a large house, on to the busy Woodhead Pass. Cross over and turn right. Just past 'The Hollins' take a road, as far as a gap in the wall left. Follow a path down to the dam of Torside Reservoir, and cross it. At the far side, turn right through the smallest of three gates, and follow the power lines towards Manchester. Just beyond the end of Rhodeswood Reservoir (see Walk 73) go straight on to a stile by a gate. Go over and turn left on to a road leading through a farm. Follow the road until it turns left sharply upwards. Here turn right to follow a rutted road down to Valehouse Reservoir at the end of which cross over the dam. Turn left at the far side, and follow the road back up to the main road. Cross over directly and ascend Chapel Brow. Turn left at the top through Tintwistle and turn right up cobbled Arnside Lane. Just before the top turn left back down to the start.

REFRESHMENTS:
The Bull, Tintwistle (tel no: 04574 3365).

Walk 93   BAKEWELL AND YOULGREAVE   10m (16km)

Maps: OS Sheets Landranger 119; Outdoor Leisure 24.

A hills and dales walk with splendid views.

Start: At 220707, the car park by the bridge, Bakewell.

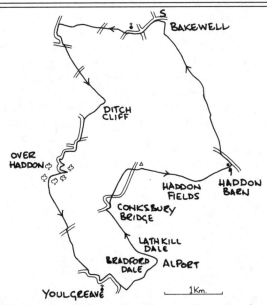

Go out of the car park, turn left over the bridge, pass the supermarket on your left, cross the A6 and go up Monyash Road to All Saints Church. Just beyond the church go sharp right and then sharp left up Parsonage Croft to open fields. Go over fields and a road to reach a second road. Turn left and left again at a T-junction. Shortly, look for a stile on the right. Cross the stile at the field corner and go diagonally left across three fields and stiles to the boundary wall of a fourth field. Follow the wall past old buildings on the right to a road. Cross the road and just to the right follow the footpath sign across two fields with the boundary left. Go over a stile by a gate (ignore the stile on the right) and along the right boundary of the next field. Go over a stile and along the left boundary to the field bottom. Go over a stile opposite and turn right along a wall to a path along the side of Ditch Cliff. At the top, the path curves left. Go over three stiles to reach a road. Turn left towards Over Haddon, and where the road turns sharp right keep straight ahead into the village street. Go right to a road junction. Take a narrow road to the left and descend steeply to the River Lathkill. Go over the bridge and ascend the track to a gate. Follow the waymarks to and through a farmyard and on to a gate with a two way signpost. Go to the left boundary wall and follow it to the road. Turn right and then left over a stile and follow the left boundary over two fields. Switch to the other side of the wall and follow it through to a walled track leading into **Youlgreave**. Pass Old Hall Farm (1630) to the main road and turn left past Conduit Head and the church.

Descend the narrow road to the right of the church and, at a sharp bend, continue down a track, over a packhorse bridge and into Bradford Dale. Follow the riverside path left to the main road at Alport. Cross straight over and walk into Lathkill Dale via a stile by a gate. An easy path up the dale reaches a road. Turn right and cross over Conksbury Bridge and ascend to a sharp right-hand bend. Here go through a stile, left, ascend the bank and follow a path to a junction of paths near the far boundary of the second field. Turn right and cross the stile, a road and another stile. Follow the left boundary for two fields, and the same line across Haddon Fields to the far boundary wall, right of the spinney. Follow the wall and then a track to reach the main A6 road by Haddon Barn with the entrance to **Haddon Hall** opposite.

Cross the main road and go left for 200 yards to a stile over the wall and to a path. At a road turn right, and then left to two paths waymarked with yellow and blue arrows. The two paths follow each other closely and it does not matter which you choose. Follow the path by the river finally crossing fields to a footbridge. Do not cross the bridge but take the path on the right to a stile and a road. Turn left to **Bakewell.**

POINTS OF INTEREST:

Youlgreave – Conduit Head was built in 1829 to supply water to the village and is still in use. The church is of Norman origin but is mainly 13/14th century.

Haddon Hall – Probably the finest example of a fortified manor house in England. Its origins go back to the 12th century. A visit is a must.

Bakewell – The town has been a market town since the granting of its charter in 1254. The river bridge has been in use since 1300 and the Information Centre was originally the 17th-century Market Hall. The church is mainly 13/14th century. There is a 9th-century Saxon cross in the churchyard and a collection of Saxon and Norman stone coffins and lids. The Museum was Parsonage House from the 15th century.

REFRESHMENTS:

The Lathkill Hotel, Over Haddon (tel no: 062 981 2501/2).
The Bulls Head, Youlgreave (tel no: 0629 636307).

Walk 94   MONYASH TO CHELMORTON   10m (16km)

Maps: OS Sheets Landranger 119; Outdoor Leisure 24.
An exhilarating walk taking in four of the higher villages.
Start: At 150665, the car park at Monyash.

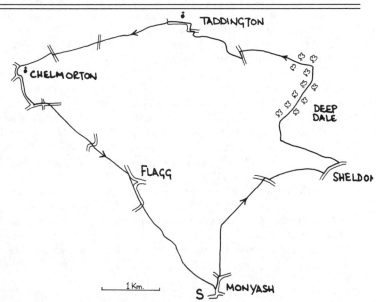

Turn left from the car park, right at the road junction and then immediately left over a stile on to a path. Follow this along the right wall to a field just past a farm and cross a stile. Head for the far end of the spinney. A stiled path, later a track, goes straight to the road. Turn right and look for a stile in the second field on the left. Cross this and go diagonally right over a series of stiles and finally a gate to reach, and cross, a stile on to a road which is 400 yards from **Sheldon**.

Go left up the road and cross a stile into the second field on the left by a signpost for Taddington. Cross the field to a stile in the left corner. Go over this and another on the immediate left. Follow the right boundary wall through a series of gates and over a stile to descend in to Deepdale. Go over the stile at the bottom, turn right and right again through a gate to follow the boundary, left, down the dale. After approximately $^1/_2$ mile (just before a rocky section) go left on a path to a junction with a rough track.

Follow the track left to reach a stile and field following the waymarkers to a road at the left of Coombs Farm. Walk the full length of the farm road to the junction with a road. Turn left and then right along a walled track. Go first right on to another walled track, turning right at the second junction and then left on to another walled track. Turn right at the second junction to reach the village street in Taddington. Go up to a three-way junction, cross the left-hand road to go along a pathway between houses leading to a minor road and a stile in to a field to the left of Rock House Farm. Go diagonally left to a stile in the far corner of the next field and a stile just left of the reservoir. Turn along the right wall and follow it to its end, crossing the centre of the final field to reach a road. A little to the right is a clear path which you follow to descend to the road by **Chelmorton** Church.

Pass the church, turn left up the road to a T-junction and turn left. Turn right at the next junction to reach a wall stile into the second field on the right. The path goes diagonally left, first to a stile in the corner by a large tree and then over three more stiles to a gate by a spinney. Go left around the mound and cross a stile, a road and a second stile. A straight line of stiles follows and you finally arrive at a wall stile adjacent to the village road. Do not cross the stile but turn through a gateway on your right to reach the far left corner of the next field and a road. Follow the road to a corner and then go straight ahead along a farm track. Where it curves left, keep ahead across three stiles to the far right corner of a field and a track. Follow the track to a sharp left turn where you keep ahead on another track. At a right-hand bend go left over a stile to a path that crosses fields and stiles to another track. This crosses fields to arrive at a path by the end of a house. The next stile exits in to the car park at **Monyash**.

POINTS OF INTEREST:

Sheldon – The Magpie Mine $1/_2$ mile from the village has the finest lead mining remains in Britain.

Chelmorton – Derbyshire's highest village (1,200ft) dominated by Chelmorton Low with two pre-historic barrows. Close by is the Five Wells Tumulus, highest megalithic tomb in Britain. The church is of Norman origin and has a collection of stone coffin lids.

Monyash – An ancient market town, with a fine 14th-century church.

REFRESHMENTS:

The Queens Arms, Taddington (tel no: 029 885 245).

Walk 95 HATHERSAGE AND STONY MIDDLETON 10m (16km)
Maps: OS Sheets Landranger 110 &119; Outdoor Leisure 24.

A walk with low and high level walking and uphill work between them.

Start: The Oddfellows car park, Hathersage.

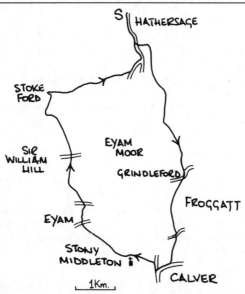

Turn right out of the car park and left at a T-junction. Follow the road to Derwent. Immediately before the river turn left up the private road to Harper Lees. Follow the river through the fields to woods where the path forks. Keep to the river path, crossing a bridge over Burbage Brook, to reach the B6521 at Grindleford. Cross the road to the right and go over a stile near a footpath sign from 1908. Go diagonally across the field to the river and a gate. Bear right and follow the wall to Froggatt Woods. Follow a path, crossing two streams and then running parallel to a wall to a stile into a field. Cross the field, passing the gate posts, to a stile and gate just short of a farm building. Turn half right to the wall corner then half left on to the farm road to Froggatt village. Walk ahead through the village, cross the river over a stone road bridge, and follow the other bank of the river to the road (B6054). Turn right to a T-junction. Turn right for 200 yards along the road to Hathersage and Sheffield and look for a footpath sign on the left pointing across an area of scrubby field to Stony Middleton. Take the path – the first part is often badly churned up by cattle and care is needed. At the stile with the bench turn left into the village. Follow The Bank and then turn right up Cliff Bottom and pass the Wesleyan Church. (Drop left to the main road and Lovers Leap Café if in need of refreshment.) At a stile follow the signposted path up the slope passing the **Boundary Stone** to a stile and a walled path left.

Cross directly to Water Lane and pass the Miners Arms to climb the road uphill. At the top cross the field on the left to the top far corner and a stile. Cross the road and follow the path up through trees. Cross three fields to reach a minor road. Turn left and after a few yards cross the wall stile on the right. Take the path across fields and a track (two stiles) to Eyam Moor. Follow the path across the moor until, dropping down through the heather, a gate is reached leading to a grassy track. The track follows a wall and then winds down the hillside to the footbridge at Stoke Ford. Keeping this side of the stream the route climbs to the right (but heading downstream), returning to the stream after passing through a small wood. Still not crossing the main stream, the path crosses a small brook to a stile. Cross an area of timber felling to a gate and a grassy track which leads to a farm track near the farm. Follow this to the right to gain a road leading down the hill, passing Hazzleford Hall, to join the Grindleford-Hathersage road. Turn left to cross the Derwent at Leadmill Bridge. Continue along the road and, 200 yards beyond the railway bridge, turn right into Oddfellows Road and return to the car park.

POINTS OF INTEREST:
The Boundary Stone – In 1666 the Great Plague came to Eyam. The village voluntarily isolated itself from the outside world and used the Boundary Stone as a place where coins could be left in payment of supplies. These were bought by the people of Stony Middleton who collected the coins from the holes in the stone where they had been immersed in vinegar to prevent infection.

REFRESHMENTS:
The Lovers Leap Café, Stony Middleton (tel no: 0433 30334), used by climbers spending the day in Middleton Vale, and by walkers.
The Miners Arms, Eyam (tel no: 0433 30853).

Walk 96   ALPORT AND ELTON   10m (16km)

Maps: OS Sheets Landranger 119; Outdoor Leisure 24.

A hills and dales walk for those preferring the quieter ways.

Start: At 222645, above the bridge at Alport.

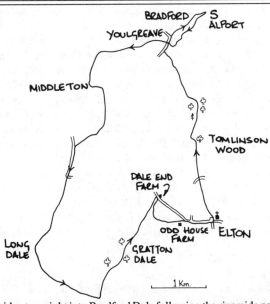

At the bridge turn right into Bradford Dale following the riverside path to a road. Cross to the right bank of the river and follow it to a footbridge. Cross this and follow the left bank to the end of a wooded section. Here a rough track ascends to Middleton. Go left off this track along the right bank of the river to cross a footbridge. Ascend steps on the far bank, turn right and shortly recross the river by another footbridge. Go right of a telegraph pole and follow the path over fields and waymarked stiles to a farm track. Cross over and follow the river to where it curves sharply left, around rocks. Go over a stile on the left, turn right along a path to a wall stile and descend to a road. Turn left and walk to a sharp bend. Go ahead here, along the hollow way between walls (**Peakway**) and, later, a farm track.

    Where the track goes between walls follow the left wall to and through gated fields to the hillside above Long Dale. A path heads diagonally left to the dale floor and a gate, and continues beyond to a gate at the dale end. Go through and left over a stile into Gratton Dale. There is no clear path here so choose the easiest route to reach the hamlet of Dale End. Turn right and then right again to follow the footpath sign direction up a house drive and right of outbuildings to a farm track curving round the hillside. Leave the track to cross a stile by a gate in the first wall on the left. Follow the left wall around a corner. Go over the wall to the far wall. Turn right along this. On reaching Oddo House Farm go left around the buildings on to a track and follow it to a road. Turn right into Elton (see Walk 84).

Turn left by the church, then first left to a gate. Go through and follow the hedge (there is no clear path) to a stile in the bottom corner of the field. From here the path is clear across several fields to a road. Cross the road and the wall stile opposite and swing right on a path, passing close to Cliff Farm, to reach a stile short of Tomlinson Wood. Go over the stile and left, parallel to the wood, then sharp right along its end. The path now crosses two fields and waymarked stiles to a rough track. Follow the track to a gateway turning left on to a path signed 'Youlgreave'. Follow the path across several fields to meet a road. Turn right and go up the road towards Youlgreave (see Walk 93). At a sharp left-hand bend go through a wall stile on the right to follow the path along the hillside to the road and the start.

POINTS OF INTEREST:
Peakway – A medieval track from Middleton to Long Dale and Pike Hall. It is referred to in a 13th-century land deed, but only two miles of the route have been identified.

REFRESHMENTS:
The Bull's Head, Youlgreave (tel no: 0629 636307).

Walk 97　　**ROWSLEY AND STANTON MOOR**　　10m (16km)

Maps: OS Sheets Landranger 119; Outdoor Leisure 24.

A fairly easy walk through trees and farmland and across moorland.

Start: At 257657, the Peacock, Rowsley.

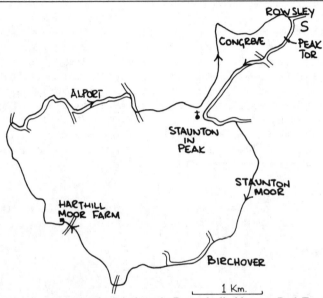

Follow the road immediately right from the Peacock climbing past Peak Tor. The road continues to Stanton village where you go left, past the Birchover turn off, to join a footpath on the right. A stile next to a gate gives access on to **Stanton Moor.**

　　Go past the tower (Stanton Monument) and continue until a road is reached. Turn right into Birchover, a tiny quaint village and an ideal resting point. The Druid Inn marks the end of the village. Go past it, along a narrow lane by the church, on to a farm track. The track bends to the left past a barn and down to the road. A few yards along the road a stile on the right side leads to a grass track. This climbs towards Hermits Cave, Stone Circle and Castle Ring on Harthill Moor (see Walk 84). Passing through a small plantation of spruce trees the track goes over a stream and heads towards Youlgreave.

At a road turn right for a few yards crossing over the river Bradford to join a footpath which follows the river to **Alport.** Once in Alport turn right and immediately left going past an old mill to the A524. Go right for a short distance to the road which climbs steeply to Stanton. Next to the church lies Stanton Hall and opposite this stiles mark the footpath towards Congreave. A stone barn is passed on the left-hand side and an iron gate marks the way. The track tends to go in a diagonally for the most part here, sloping down to a stile in the right-hand corner. Turn right on the lane and go uphill a short distance to where a footpath on the left continues on the hillside back to Rowsley.

POINTS OF INTEREST:
Stanton Moor – Various stone circles are found upon the moor along with remains and burial mounds dating back to the Bronze Age.
Alport – Between the early 17th and 19th centuries this was a thriving industrial settlement based on lead mining.

REFRESHMENTS:
The Druid Inn, Birchover (tel no: 062 988 302).
The Peacock, Rowsley (tel no: 0629 733518).

Walk 98   **BACK TOR**   11m (17.5km)

Maps: OS Sheets Landranger 110; Outdoor Leisure 1.

A fairly serious walk with a short stretch of steep climbing in the early stages. Not a walk to be undertaken in bad visibility.

Start: At 168939, the Kings Tree car park, Derwent Reservoir.

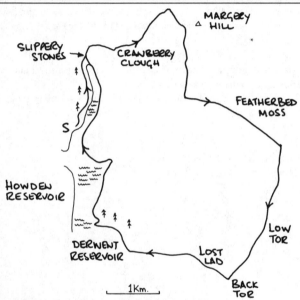

Leave Kings Tree by the gate and follow the forestry road across the ford and up through trees. Go left at a fork and continue to the packhorse bridge at Slippery Stones (see Walk 81). Cross over and bear left past sheepfolds to a wooden footbridge. Cross and go right to pass a sign to Floush Inn. Follow the arrow to cross a small stream at the junction of Bull Clough and Cranberry Clough, and climb the path steeply up the shoulder of the hill. The path bears left across the top of an old land slip and goes high along the side of Bull Clough before swinging right to continue climbing, more gently, towards Cut Gate. The path is well-defined and marked by cairns at intervals. Continue until the ground levels after a further two cairns and turn right at the second cairn to follow a staked path to the trig. point on Margery Hill. The rocks of the next objective on this walk, Back Tor, can be seen just above the line of the moor in the middle distance and in line with the edge overlooking the Derwent Valley. To get to Back Tor, the route has to firstly swing round the head waters of Abbey Brook. Now walk along the Edge path towards the Tor, losing sight of it for a while. As it comes into view again on the high point of the edge a small low cairn marks the place to leave the path. Looking left the line of a track can be seen leading across to a small grough or gully, one of the small streams that forms Abbey Brook. Follow this line to the stream.

The stream, no more than a stride wide, spreads to form a wide boggy area of light-coloured grass and reeds. Pass this by crossing a smaller stream cut deep into the peat and keeping to the left-hand edge of the boggy area. Follow the course of the stream as it flows down a gradually deepening trough until a pair of shooting butts can be seen on the left. Shortly afterwards the path leaves the stream and rises to the left to bring Back Tor in to view again. Continue on the path, through the heather, towards a patch of bare ground. Before reaching the bare ground you will pass a post and a cairn where our route joins a path from the left. Bear right across the bare ground to follow a path to, and over, a brow. Now follow an old drainage ditch to Back Tor. From the Tor cross to the top of Lost Lad with its cairn and topograph. Follow the path roughly north-west from the topograph, keeping left where it forks and continuing down the hillside in a shallow gully or old drainage ditch. A broad path leads to the left across flat ground but our path stays with the ditch and follows it across a small stream in a dip to a stile over a wire fence. Turn right down the path which becomes a vehicle track leading steeply down to trees and the service road alongside the reservoir. Turn right and follow the road back to Slippery Stones. Cross the river and turn left to return to Kings Tree.

REFRESHMENTS:
A *snack bar* is open at Fairholme picnic site and car park during the summer.

Maps: OS Sheets Landranger 119; Outdoor Leisure 24.
A very varied walk, part gritstone and part limestone.
Start: At 270624, the Darley Bridge Picnic Site.

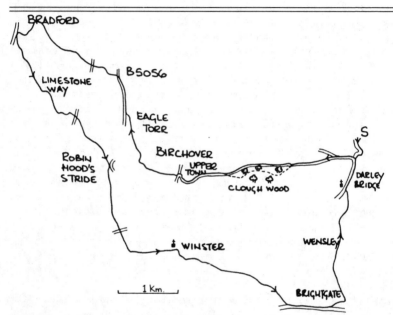

Turn right out of the car park, over Darley Bridge (see walk 51) and first right opposite the Post Office. Go left at the fork and continue to the wood. Take the lower path past the ruin of **Watt's Engine House** and through Clough Wood. Continue to Uppertown, Birchover. Turn left, then right on a path signed 'Eagle Tor'. Go down a field then right of a hedge, not through the gate. Go over a stile and along Birchover Wood. Go over a stile and down to Rocking Stone Farm. Turn right over a stile and go down to a path junction. Go through the right-hand gate. Keep to the wall, bear right through a gateway and over a field towards the houses at Eagle Tor. Go down a bank, over a stream and on to a road. Turn left, then right on to the B5056. Go along it for 800 yards to a Public Bridleway just before Stoney Ley Lodge. Follow it to a bridge. Go uphill and right around a mound and a copse. Turn left up a bank and across a field to a gate on to a road. Go through the gate ahead, follow a fence, through another gate, then past caravans on to a track past a farm. Go down to the River Bradford. Turn left and follow the river to a road. Go left to a path signposted and waymarked by yellow arrows (the Limestone Way). At the Harthill Moor Farm track ignore a left turn over a bridge and continue to the farm. Turn right to a road and take the footpath opposite to **Robin Hood's Stride.**

Go left of the rocks, following the Old Portway (see Walk 31). At the road go ahead to a lane (not sharp right to Dudwood Farm). This crosses a road continuing as the Limestone Way. At a farm track turn left on to a footpath. Go over stiles to a road, cross and continue, opposite and slightly right, over more stiles to **Winster** church.

Turn right from the churchyard. As the road bends right, take a wide alley, left. Keep left at the top on a small road, turn right by Birch View cottage and left along the road at the top. Ahead is a footpath signed 'Bonsall', by the side of Headlands Cottage. After two stiles, bear right uphill then left around the hillside, then uphill again and round Luntor Rocks and a wood. Go over the next stile, then over a stile in the wall, right. A path follows the wall, left, for three fields. At an arrow pointing back ascend diagonally across four fields. Bear left along the wall heading for a tall post with an arrow. Turn uphill following the arrow to the far corner of a large field and a road. Turn left to Brightgate. Just past Brightgate Farm on the left go over a stile by a gate. The Right of Way goes to the right along the wall, over a stile and left down a hill with capped lead mine shafts. At a low, broken wall to the right, go down to a large gap by a mine shaft. Go down to a stile, ahead to the next stile and down through a gap in the wall. Bear left to a stile, cross the track to Wensley, go over a stile in a high wall, up over the brow of the hill and down into Wensley Dale. Cross the dale, go over a stile opposite, to the left of a cliff and follow the wall up to the next field. Cross diagonally right to a stile. Go ahead to a road, cross and go down a path to South Darley School. At a road, to the right, go right, down the main road through the village of Darley Bridge and back to the start.

POINTS OF INTEREST:
Watt's Engine House – The Millclose Mine, Derbyshire's largest ever lead mine.
Robin Hood's Stride – Also known as Mock Beggar's Hall, a gritstone outcrop, site of Romano-British huts on the route of the Old Portway.
Winster – Lead-mining centre in the 18th century, the mine owners living on the main street, the miners in the cottages on the bank.

REFRESHMENTS:
The Three Stags Head , Darley Bridge (tel no: 0629 732358).
The Square and Compass , Darley Bridge (tel no: 0629 733255). Morning coffee.
The Bowling Green , Winster (tel no: 0629 88219).

Walk 100   LATHKILL DALE   12m (19km)

Maps: OS Sheets Landranger 119; Outdoor Leisure 24.

A walk that includes a length of the Lathkill Dale, noted for its scenery.

Start: At 150665, the car park, Monyash.

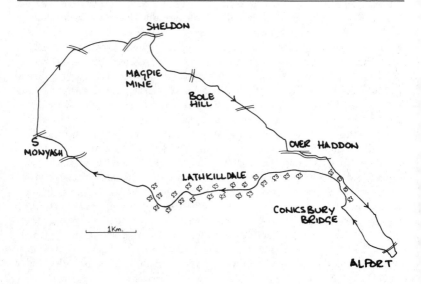

Turn left from the car park, right at the road junction and immediately left over a stile on to a path. Follow the right wall to a field just past a farm and cross a stile heading for the trees at the far end of the field. Continue along a path with stiles which becomes a track to a road. Turn right and at the second field on the left cross a stile and walk diagonally right over a series of stiles and finally a gate to a stile in the field corner and the road. Walk into Sheldon (see Walk 94) and take the walled path by a telegraph post adjacent to 'P Gregory, Engineers'. Cross two narrow fields to a gate, in the far right corner of a third field, to a walled track. Go over a stile in the left wall and follow the clear path across the field towards Magpie Mine. To visit the mine go straight ahead across next field. Our walk continues by turning left along the wall to a stile on the right of a gate. Go over and over another in the far right wall by a thorn bush. Turn left to a walled track descending to the road through Kirk Dale. Cross the road and the stile opposite and veer right to ascend the slope on an indistinct path that leads to the right edge of the trees and a waymarked gate. Follow the waymarks over a stile, across a field to a further stile and then along the left boundary to the next stile. Go diagonally left in a straight line to cross three fields, a road and further fields to reach a track. Soon, cross a stile on the left to follow the previous line across three fields to another track leading into Over Haddon.

Turn left at the road, first right, then left to go along the village street to the Lathkill Hotel. At the wall end in front of the hotel is a stile by a footpath sign and two paths across fields. Take the right-hand path which follows a fairly straight line across fields to a road, two more fields and then a yard and farm buildings. Go through the gate at the far end of the yard on to a rough track – part of the Old Portway (see Walk 31) – descending to the road at Alport. To see the hamlet cross to a minor road opposite, turn right along the street and come back to the main road and the bridge. Cross the road to a stile by a gate and walk into the lower reaches of Lathkill Dale. A pathway across fields arrives at a road. Go over Conksbury Bridge and continue along the right bank of the river. Note the clarity of the water and the numerous trout. Where a minor road comes in from the right, turn up it for a few yards and then turn left along a wide path which was originally an access road to the old lead mine further on. After passing through a lovely wooded section the path becomes rough as it passes through a rocky section with evidence on the hillside of old mining and quarrying activities. The path then reaches the road outside Monyash (see Walk 94). Cross the road to the left to follow a footpath curving left around field boundaries to reach the road junction where the walk began.

REFRESHMENTS:
The Lathkill Hotel, Over Haddon (tel no: 062 981 2501).